This book belongs to

If this book has taken a road trip of its own,
I would be forever grateful if you could reunite us.
Good karma will come your way!

This is an Axel & Ash book, part of the 'insert your story' series. First Published in 2016. This is the second edition Luxe White Cover.

We would absolutely love to see pictures of all your wild roadtrip adventures. Tag us on social media:

@axelandash #lifesaroadtrip #axelandash
www.axelandash.com | info@axelandash.com

Publisher Axel & Ash
Creative Directors / Writers Ashleigh Powell & Hanna Axelsson Sahlen
Art Director & Designer Jessica Wells
Junior Designer Jillian Sun
Editor / Writer Luanne Shneier
Contributors Inga Wendelin & Jordyn Christensen.
Photography by Amelia Fullarton, Annica Olsson, Ashley Batz, Ashley Hollender, Ashleigh Powell, Caitlin Miers, Chase Baird, Eilis Yates, Ivan & Beth Hodge, Hanna Axelsson Sahlen, James Campbell, Jenelle Kappe, Jordan Hammond, Joseph Vella, Kim Leuenberger, Kym Pham, Lenita Storeide, Matthew Ridenour, Mark Clinton, Max Papendieck, Mimi Elashiry, Ming Nomchong, Nicole Kinner, Oscar Nilsson, Parker Hilton, Paul Krol, Petra Švecová (Vostálová), Thomas Flensted- Jensen, Rachel Goldfarb, Ruby Hollinger, Sabine Eva Stepinski, Vivianne Flores, Zoë Timmers.

ISBN: 978-0-9874493-3-7 (Luxe White Cover)
Original ISBN: 978-0-9874493-2-0 (Brown cover)

Printed in China through Red Planet Print Management.

life's a ROADTRIP

Road trip   roadtrip

*A long distance journey on the road, typically travelled
by automobile, often unplanned or impromptu.*

I DON'T KNOW WHERE I'M GOING FROM HERE, BUT I PROMISE

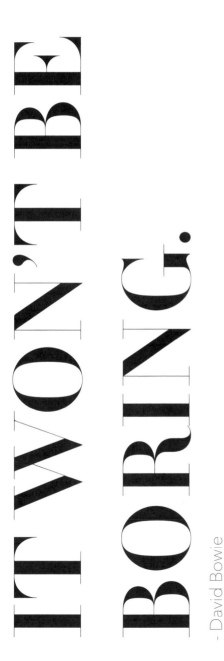

IT WON'T BE BORING.

- David Bowie

Wild, curious and carefree. The world is our playground and there's no better way to feel at one with the earth than hitting the road and exploring it on wheels.

Whether it's a weekend getaway, heading to your favourite festival, crossing borders, beach hopping to chase an endless summer, or driving across an entire country - a road trip is always a good idea!

There's something magical about wandering at your own pace, spending the night wherever feels right, and waking up somewhere new each day. Why stay in one place when you can choose a new backyard every night? Dense forests, enchanting mountain views or a beach paradise to dive into when the sun rises - the choice is all yours! Add your best friends, an epic playlist and a tank full of wanderlust, and you've got a recipe for an unforgettable adventure.

'Life's a Roadtrip' has been designed to awaken the road tripper inside you, and is filled with inspiring stories from free-spirited travellers, beautiful photography, lists of hidden locations to discover, quotes to push your wanderlust buttons, and a scavenger hunt to add an extra dash of quirk to your trip.

To capture your favourite moments forever, you'll find eight journaling chapters (each for a new journey, or combine them to record one long adventure), where you'll be prompted to jot down all the little things that make a road trip so memorable: the characters you meet along the way, the unexpected towns you stumble upon, the sunsets you'll never forget, and the special bonds created with your travel buddies.

Life on the road ignites your spirit and your soul, opening the door to the most incredible, weird and unforgettable stories. So what are you waiting for? Life goes by in an instant. Feel the pulse of the world, explore, adventure and get wonderfully lost in the magic of it all. It's time to insert YOUR story! See you on the road! ♥

with love, Axel&Ash

at the
end of the
day, your
feet should
be dirty,
your hair
messy
& your
eyes sparkling

ADVENTURE
awaits...

I GOT THIS BOOK FROM

DATE

IT MADE ME THINK

ROAD TRIPS I'M DREAMING OF GOING ON

ROAD TRIPS I'VE DONE SO FAR

I LOVE BEING ON THE ROAD BECAUSE

MY DREAM ROAD TRIP CAR

My story right now...

MY DAYS ARE SPENT

I'M DREAMING OF

I'M PASSIONATE ABOUT

I NEED TO

I'M TERRIFIED OF

I'M GRATEFUL FOR

I SPEND TOO MUCH TIME

I SPEND TOO LITTLE TIME

I WANT TO LEARN

I KEEP PUTTING OFF

PEOPLE WHO INSPIRE ME

I CAN'T WAIT TO

'We age not by years, but by stories.' - Pavana

Road Trip Bucket list

Remember when you were a kid and had all the time in the world to be carefree and silly with your friends? A road trip is one big adventure and it's all about the people you meet, the places you see, the wild things you do and the stories you hear along the way. Be spontaneous, get out of your comfort zone, detour, embrace those moments and let your inner child run free...

Find a local market and sample produce.

Be the pinnacle of a human pyramid.

Find a hidden water hole and go for a skinny dip.

Learn the story of a local busker.

Visit a random factory and ask for a tour.

Hug a tree and show gratitude for nature.

Get a photo with a local at each stop and learn an interesting fact from them.

Walk through a fountain.

Introduce yourself to three strangers.

Swan dive off a jetty.

Start a conga line in a bar.

Pick a yoga pose and hold it in the middle of a crowd.

Get invited to a stranger's house for a meal.

Go for a swim at sunrise.

Listen to a podcast while driving.

Write your name with rocks in the sand.

Cook a meal under the moonlight.

Carve your initials (somewhere discreet but special).

Have a campfire and roast marshmallows.

Make a music video - sing at the top of your lungs and dance like no one is watching.

Spot a native animal.

Pull over to play at a local playground.

Wash someone else's windows at a gas station.

Plant a seed.

Spend a night sharing stories under the stars.

Stick your head out the window and feel the wind blowing on your face.

Follow a random handmade or billboard sign.

Tell a bunch of your best jokes over a meal - especially the bad ones.

Find a natural hot spring and melt away.

Get a picture in the middle of a deserted road.

Stop at a local farm and buy some fresh produce.

Try a new dessert.

Visit a museum or art gallery.

Personally compliment the chef at a cafe or restaurant you visit.

Climb a tree.

Use a free trial pass to a fitness, dance or art class you've never tried before.

Pull over next to a beautiful field of flowers and take a picture running through them.

Fall asleep on the beach.

Spot a shooting star.

Pat an animal.

Create your own on-the-road recipe and name the dish.

Pick fruit straight from the tree.

Lie down in the grass and watch the clouds pass by.

Practice your handstand.

Read a local newspaper.

Shower under a waterfall.

Talk to an animal.

Visit a vintage store.

Learn something new.

Meditate on a beach.

there is no time to be bored in a world as beautiful as this

N° 1

THE PEOPLE.
THE JOURNEY.
THE ADVENTURES.

ONE

FROM

TO

START DATE

END DATE

Date:
Place:

THIS TRIP STARTED FROM

I'M ROAD TRIPPING WITH

TIME WE PLANNED TO LEAVE   TIME WE ACTUALLY LEFT

WE WERE WAITING ON

THINGS I FORGOT TO PACK

WE'VE NAMED OUR CAR

MAKE   MODEL   SEATS

IT BELONGS TO   I THINK IT WILL LAST THE JOURNEY   YES / NO

I WAS INSPIRED TO GO ON THIS TRIP BY

MY DRAWING OF THE ROUTE...

get ready for this wild ride...

THE FIRST DAY WAS

TOWNS WE STOPPED IN   PLACES WE ATE

WE DROVE FOR

THE DRIVER WAS

FOR DINNER WE   PS. Don't forget to
                                                 reset the odometer
WE SLEPT

THE ADVENTURES. PEOPLE. THE JOURNEY.

N° 1

MY CURRENT THOUGHTS

let's get out of this town,
drive out of the city,
away from the crowds.
- Taylor Swift

Date:
Place:

TODAY IS   WHICH IS DAY   OF THE ROAD TRIP

I WOKE UP AT

MY BED WAS

FOR BREAKFAST, I

                                   COFFEE WAS   GOOD / BAD / NON-EXISTENT

TODAY'S ADVENTURES

AT NIGHT, WE

WE ARE SLEEPING IN

WHICH FEELS

                             WE ARE   KMS / MILES, FROM THE LAST STOP

WHAT I'M LOVING ABOUT BEING ON THE ROAD

Check out a local
gig, theatre or
sports game in
a town you're
passing through.

THE WHEELS

📷 *snap happy*

SMELLS LIKE

LOOKS LIKE

RUNS LIKE

BEST FEATURE

THE CREW

Pilot _____

Co-pilot _____

D.J. _____

Singer

Comedian

Always hungry

Smallest bladder

Date:
Place:

TODAY IS DAY   OF THE ROAD TRIP

RIGHT NOW, I'M

THE SCENERY IS

MY IMPRESSION OF THIS PLACE

LOCAL SECRETS I'VE STUMBLED ACROSS

HAIRIEST MOMENT SO FAR

RULES WE'VE BROKEN

A RANDOM FACT I'VE LEARNED

TODAY WAS SPENT

THINGS DIDN'T GO TO PLAN WHEN

FROM HERE WE ARE TRAVELLING...

Currently...

ON REPEAT

TEXTING

WEARING

OBSESSED WITH

CAN'T STOP SINGING

READING

CRAVING

SMELLING

MISSING

DAYDREAMING ABOUT

LOOKING TO FIND

I SEE OUT THE WINDOW

DRINKING

MY PHONE HAS   % BATTERY LEFT

THIS HURTS

THE WEATHER IS

MY SUNGLASSES ARE

I'M WONDERING

MY FAVOURITE HUMAN IS

BECAUSE

IMAGE: @VIVIANLEEFIRS

Date:

Place:

IT IS NOW DAY   OF THE TRIP, AND WE ARE CURRENTLY

AROUND ME I CAN SEE

SUNRISES AND SUNSETS I'VE SEEN SO FAR

THE MOST BREATHTAKING WAS

FAVOURITE STRETCH OF ROAD WE'VE BEEN ON

TONIGHT WE ARE SLEEPING IN A... TENT / HOSTEL / HOTEL / CAR / AIRBNB / UNDER THE STARS

SPONTANEOUS PITSTOPS

THE STRANGEST ENCOUNTER

Go to page 260 and start jotting down your bucket list.

Come with me
WHERE DREAMS
ARE BORN & TIME
IS NEVER PLANNED.

- Peter Pan

Date:

Place:

I'M CURRENTLY

THE JOURNEY HERE WAS

IT TOOK   HOURS TO DRIVE HERE, AND WE'RE STAYING FOR   DAYS

WE CAME HERE TO

THE SEASON IS

THE BEST ADVICE WE WERE GIVEN ABOUT THIS PLACE

THE STYLE & VIBE HERE

IT'S FAMOUS FOR

SOMETHING I FOUND HERE THAT I CAN'T GET AT HOME

The Best...

CAFE

JOKE

OFF THE BEATEN TRACK

PICTURE TAKEN

MORNING

DAY

NIGHT

PERSONALITY I MET

SONG

CATCHPHRASE

SNACK

ROAD SIGN

SIGHTS I'VE SEEN

WIFI CONNECTION

N° 1

SOMETHING I LEARNED ABOUT MYSELF

I WILL NEVER BE THE SAME BECAUSE

MY ROAD TRIP SUMMED UP IN WORDS

Write, draw, scribble, notes, pictures, tickets, receipts...

27.6648° N / 81.5158° W

rolling on
SUNSHINE

In 2012, two creative souls destined to live a wild and carefree existence traded the comforts of the modern world for life on the road. In their bright orange 1976 Volkswagen Kombi named 'Sunshine', James and Rachel set off into the unknown to create what they call 'The Idle Theory' - their secret recipe to a well-balanced, fulfilled life.

idle theory bus

What started as a deep longing to travel and explore the world, turned into a boundless adventure and an enviable lifestyle.

After feeling unfulfilled in the hustle and bustle of Los Angeles, high school sweethearts Rachel, a writer and illustrator, and James, a filmmaker and photographer, felt the desire to create a healthier balance between time spent working, pursuing passions and what they call being idle - simply just 'doing nothing'.

They quit their jobs, sold all their belongings, moved out of their apartment and moved into their quirky hippie van full-time. Unsure of where the journey would take them or when it would come to an end, they hit the road to seek out a quality of life that modern society wasn't offering them.

Fast forward four years, James and Rachel are still on the go exploring every corner of the United States. They spend their days discovering untouched landscapes, daydreaming under the bare sky, bathing in cold water creeks and sleeping under the stars. They've found a perfect balance between work, travel, art and reconnecting with the earth.

Artists at heart, they love to capture the beauty of the world and share their alternate ways of seeking a fulfilling existence. When money is scarce, they work on farms or freelance their creative talents to earn just enough to move on to the next place.

Along the way, these curious wanderers have learned that the less they have, the happier they are, and that it's experiences - not possessions – that make life worth living.

WOW, FOUR YEARS ON THE ROAD...WHAT WERE YOU DOING BEFOREHAND?

James We both met in English class in high school. I then went to film school in LA and got a job in San Diego making surf videos. Rachel kept telling me that we needed to get out and go explore the world. I had this beautiful girl in my life who wanted to travel in a van, you couldn't really pass that up. That's not something that happens twice.

Rachel Before we left California, we spent a year on the road together and some time on farms. I knew that was the life I wanted to live. We went to LA because it was James's dream and I didn't want to stand in the way. When we got down there I was working as a waitress by night and writing during the day - I decided I just couldn't do it anymore.

WHAT SPARKED YOU TO TAKE OFF INDEFINITELY?

James Working behind a desk, we really wanted to go out into the world, hike and touch things. Our theory of life is to work for what you need but not more than that.

Rachel Luxuries in life are nice, but we wanted to eliminate 'wants' and how much we work for extras. When we went out on the road, we found ourselves with a lot of time for the things that we always dreamed of doing - now we can do a lot of those things. Our parents thought we were crazy, and my dad thought my college education was a bad return on investment (laughs).

HOW DID SUNSHINE JOIN YOUR FAMILY?

James I was visiting Rachael in college and she told me about this bus that was parked in the Kmart parking lot with a 'For Sale' sign - she'd been eyeing it off all semester. I took it for a test drive and it was love at first sight. We put in new drawers, a new countertop and my parents old 1970s Coleman stove - she's still very original! >

Life on the Road

SO YOU'VE BEEN ON THE ROAD NOW SINCE 2012, WHAT HAVE BEEN SOME OF THE HIGHLIGHTS? *Rachel* Being in touch with the natural world is a highlight in general. Living in the van makes us hyperaware of all of our surroundings, like the phases of the moon. I've learned that when there is a full moon, I don't sleep very well. In eastern Nevada, we were on a dirt back road and we didn't see anyone else for close to two weeks. We would stop in the middle of the desert and hike out into the silence that was almost deafening. You got lost in how quiet it was - every sound you made sounded like you were echoing into the universe.

James We loved Idaho and Montana, there are a lot of hot springs up there. When you don't have a shower, a hot spring is like heaven on earth - better than any shower you could ever take!

YOU SLEEP IN SOME REMOTE SPOTS. DO YOU EVER FEEL UNSAFE? *Rachel* James knows a lot about survival in the wilderness, so I've learned lots too. We feel more uncomfortable when we are camping near a city! People scare us more sometimes than space does. I'd prefer to be in the middle of nowhere than in the city.

WHAT ARE THE BEST THINGS ABOUT BEING ON THE ROAD? *Rachel* Ultimate freedom. When you don't have anything, you don't have anything to loose. You don't feel inhibited, because what's the worst thing that could happen? In a way it's strange, living in an unstructured way is more comfortable because I feel like I'm in more control of my life.

WHAT ARE THE THREE CRAZIEST JOBS YOU'VE HAD ALONG THE WAY? *Rachel* We worked at a goat dairy farm and it was kid season, so there were all these little baby goats everywhere. We also shovelled a fountain for six weeks - we literally dug gravel out of this fountain in a shopping centre for eight hours a day. It was really weird!

James We've harvested chestnuts, peaches and grapes, and worked in wineries too. The longest we've worked in one place is six weeks and then we're ready to leave. Now, we make more commercials or videos for businesses and non-profit organisations.

YOU'RE BOTH VERY CREATIVE, HOW DOES LIFE ON THE ROAD FULFIL YOU IN THAT SENSE? *James* I had a dream job making films back in San Diego, but I wasn't really able to bring Rachel into it. Branching out on the road and creating Idle Theory Bus as its own art project, has allowed us to be artists together which is really cool.

Rachel I've always wanted to have a life which is a beautiful piece of art in itself, and I think we've gotten to build that. It's really cool to live that way - in a way that you think is beautiful.

LET'S TALK ABOUT YOUR CONCEPT, 'THE IDLE THEORY'. YOU BELIEVE THAT THERE ARE THREE DIVISIONS OF TIME: IDLE, WORK AND LEISURE. WHAT IS THE MESSAGE YOU'RE AIMING TO SHARE? *James* We are definitely overworked as a society, we work as a means of defining ourselves. We want to share the message that you don't have to work so much to enjoy life. You don't have to be looked upon as lazy because you don't work for money like that. We developed a theory that there are three divisions of time. 'work': the time spent on survival, 'idle': the time spent doing nothing, 'leisure': the time spent on passions.

Rachel The message we preach is to take time to do things that you love that don't involve money - your passions! Taking time to do nothing is just as important. We have found that we actively do nothing. For some people there's a fear of doing nothing - you don't have to justify your existence by being busy. We don't think you should be idle all the time, but it's something that is important to allow yourself to do nothing.

WHAT IS YOUR IDLE TIME? *Rachel* Not having plans, having no structure. Simply sitting down, looking out, not talking and being in the moment.

WHAT'S THE MOST IMPORTANT THING THAT YOU'VE LEARNED ON THE ROAD? *James* Appreciating the small things. Looking at things for what they really are, instead of what you think they will be.

Rachel I've learned that I can have a lot of close friendships with people on the go. In a strange way, this lifestyle really works for me - I love meeting a person on the road, people are vulnerable and share a lot when they're travelling. I'm okay with making a friend and not knowing if I'll see them again.

WHAT DO YOU MISS MOST FROM YOUR 'OLD LIFE'? *Rachel* Watching movies, we never watch them now. We feel very out of touch with what's going on. I miss being able to have a library of books... and an oven! But I don't think there's that much else that I miss, it's very comfortable for us.

TELL US ABOUT THE MOST BEAUTIFUL ROAD YOU'VE TRAVELLED ON? *Rachel* Lizard Head Pass on the way to Telluride in Colorado, near the Rocky Mountains. The sand hills in Nebraska also captured my imagination - you can travel in a straight road all day and just be surrounded by grass.

THE BEST PLACE YOU'VE SLEPT IN? *Rachel* We were in Big Bend last winter in Texas - we don't really follow the news so we didn't know about it, but there was this huge meteor shower one night. We were up 'til midnight watching shooting stars. It was so much more magical as we didn't know it was going to happen.

ANY SECRET SWIMMING HOLES YOU CAN SHARE WITH US? *James* Phelps Lake, in the Tetons in Wyoming. There's a sweet rock jump into the lake - it's about 30 feet, it's intense!

TELL US ABOUT SOME OF YOUR BEST HIKES? *James* We went through Glacier National Park (Montana) - we hiked the whole thing and it took over an entire week. It was pretty spectacular. We also

idle theory bus

went to the Maroon Bells in Colorado this year, there's a hike that goes over four passes - you're alpine the entire time.

WHAT ADVICE DO YOU HAVE FOR OTHER PEOPLE WHO WANT TO FOLLOW YOUR FOOTSTEPS? *James* I'd say don't get to caught up in your plans, just be open and say yes. Keep your plans loose, allow them to change, and try not to see more than three things a day. Say yes to whatever comes along and listen to your gut. Keep your expectations low and you will always be happy!

SO WHAT'S NEXT FOR THE SUNSHINE CREW? *Rachel* Next is to drive north in the summer and then south in the winter. We're writing a book at the moment, 'Orange is Optimism'. It's been a dream of mine to be a writer and getting the book printed this year will be a dream come true. ♥

See Rachel & James on Instagram @idletheorybus

N⁰ 2

THE ADVENTURES. THE JOURNEY. LE.

TWO

FROM

TO

START DATE

END DATE

BEFORE
we hit the road

THE IDEA FOR THIS ROAD TRIP CAME FROM

WE STARTED TO PLAN IT WHEN

WITH THE GOAL TO

I'M MOST EXCITED ABOUT

BEFORE TAKING OFF, I NEED TO ORGANISE

THE PLANNED ROUTE IS...

PACKING LIST

'Embrace uncertainty. Some of the most beautiful chapters in our lives won't have a title until much later.' - Bob Goff

MY DESCRIPTION OF IT

OWNED BY

I TRUST IT WILL

I JUMPED IN THE CAR AT   RUNNING   LATE   /   EARLY   /   JUST ON TIME

BECAUSE

THE ROAD TRIP CREW

BEST THINGS THEY'VE BROUGHT ALONG

DESIGNATED DRIVER

RIDING SHOTGUN

BACKSEAT BANDITS

FIRST TUNE PLAYED

CHOSEN BY

FIRST CONVERSATION

MY FEELINGS AS WE DROVE OFF

Date:
Place:

FIRST DESTINATION

THE ROAD TO GET HERE WAS

THIS PLACE IN WORDS

PEOPLE I SPOKE TO

RIGHT NOW, I'M IN LOVE WITH

Moments here...

Feathers, shells, sticks, fairy lights or wild flowers. Decorate the car inside & out with keepsakes you've found along the way...

things...

I DREAM OF

I WISH

I PONDER

THAT INSPIRE ME

I WANT TO LEARN

I WANT TO EXPERIENCE

I WANT TO ACHIEVE

THAT MAKE MY HEART JUMP

Date:

Place:

TODAY IS DAY   OF THE ROAD TRIP AND I'M CURRENTLY

I'M GOING TO BE HERE FOR

THE BED I SLEPT IN LAST NIGHT

MY MORNING

MY AFTERNOON

MY EVENING

EMOTIONS THAT DESCRIBE ME RIGHT NOW

On this trip...

I LAUGHED AT

I WAS RIGHT ABOUT

I WAS WRONG ABOUT

I TASTED

I LEARNED

I GOT TO KNOW

I WAS HAPPY WHEN

I WILL ALWAYS REMEMBER

Date:

Place:

RIGHT NOW, I'M IN

I'VE BEEN ON THE ROAD FOR

I'M LOVING

IN THE CAR, I ENJOY

THE SIGHTS WE'VE SEEN ALONG THE WAY

THINGS I WANT TO SEE AND DO HERE

I'M GOING TO BE HERE FOR

AND SLEEP AT

DISTANCE WE'VE COVERED SO FAR

THE LONGEST STRETCH WAS

I LIKE THAT THIS PLACE IS

I CAN'T WAIT TO

BIGGEST DECISION TODAY

BEST DECISION TODAY

BEST MOMENT IN THE LAST 24 HOURS

... AND THE WORST

The Last...

DRINK I HAD

THOUGHT I HAD

BATHROOM I VISITED

THING I LAUGHED AT

SHOES I WORE

RECIPE I LEARNED

PERSON I WAS SAD TO SAY GOODBYE TO

STORY I HEARD

MEAL I ATE

SENTENCE I SPOKE

TIME I WORKED

PERSON I ADORED

ANIMAL I SAW

SHOWER I USED

TIME I FELT STRESSED

NEW WORD I LEARNED

PROMISE I MADE

GAS STATION WE STOPPED AT

SUNSET I CAUGHT

KISS

THIS MADE ME SMILE

adventure

Date:

Place:

TODAY IS   MON / TUES / WED / THURS / FRI / SAT / SUN / I FORGET

IT'S DAY _____ OF THE TRIP AND THE ODOMETER READS _____

THE JOURNEY SO FAR HAS BEEN _____

_____

I WOKE UP SURROUNDED BY _____

_____

SMELLING _____

SEEING _____

FEELING _____

TASTING _____

RIGHT NOW, I AM _____

_____

THIS PLACE _____

_____

_____

THE QUEST HERE IS TO

'Ten years from now, make sure you can say that you chose your life, you didn't settle for it.' - Mandy Hale

SUMMARY

LOCALS I MET

HIGHLIGHT OF THE TRIP

SIGHTS I SAW

NOOKS I'VE FOUND

SONGS I SANG

PERSONALITIES I'VE ADORED

PLACES I'VE DANCED

PRETTIEST THING I'VE SEEN

FUNNIEST MOMENT

WORST MOMENT

WE ALMOST DIED WHEN

WE WERE SURPRISED

WE GOT LOST *(whose fault?)*

A MISCOMMUNICATION

THE WEATHER HAS BEEN

MOST FREQUENT DRIVER

BEST LOCATION

TEMPER LOST

SNACKS WE ATE

THE CAR IS CURRENTLY   SPOTLESS / NEEDING A CLEAN / A MESS / A HOARDER'S DREAM snap happy

Write down, scribble notes, pictures, tickets, receipts...

Nº 2

Chasing WAVES

There's nothing quite like that soul-stirring feeling of freedom you get from being on the road, whether it's a few days or a few hours, solo, or with your best friends. Every day is a road trip for Australian surf photographer Cait Miers, who heads out each day with a coffee in hand, the wind in her hair and sand beneath her pedals to do what she loves most.

At first glance, Cait is your quintessential surfer chick. But beneath her sun-kissed skin and golden locks, this down-to-earth 23 year-old is living a life many of us could only dream of. Having turned her obsession with the ocean and her love for travel into a living, Cait ventures to some of the world's most beautiful locations to shoot for the biggest names in the surfing industry.

Her whirlwind career, or her 'little circus' as she describes it, has led her to work with iconic labels Billabong, Roxy and O'Neill and the likes of six-time world surfing champion, Stephanie Gilmore. She's even started her own swimwear label, Zea - an

impressive list of achievements for someone who left school unsure of what to do.

Having grown up in the sleepy coastal town of Mornington, being on the road and connected to the ocean forms the essence of who Cait is. She grew up swimming, surfing and camping around Australia with her adventurous family, even missing a term of school as a nine year old to explore the country in a caravan.

She'd never planned to be a photographer, but always knew that no matter what she did for a living, she had to be immersed in the surf culture that she lives and breathes. Cait describes her ongoing

love affair with the ocean as the only constant thing in her life. *"Every time I'm in the ocean, it's just so natural to be there. It's like this comforting cushion - it's always there for you."*

Her adventures on the road have since led her on some epic journeys, and have included cruising in a convertible to secluded locations around Bali, driving her grandma's car in convoy with her best friends to uncover hidden surf spots on the East Coast of Australia, and waking up in a car on the beach at a summer music festival. Wherever she is headed, Cait has her camera on the dashboard, ready to pull over and capture every beautiful moment.

For Cait, being on the road is all about blissing out, being surrounded by nature and watching the world go by in slow motion. Yet it's her morning surf ritual, where she hits the road with her best friends to chase the waves at her hometown beach, that inspires her the most.

CAIT, YOUR LIFE SOUNDS LIKE A DREAM. HOW WOULD YOU DESCRIBE IT IN THREE WORDS? Spontaneous, adventurous, happy.

WHAT DO YOU LOVE MOST ABOUT BEING ON THE ROAD? I don't know why, but I love driving. I think it's because I'm a 'slow it down' kinda girl, meaning I play music that moves me and I really feel free when I drive. Driving to the surf is one of my favourite things to do. I crank up the music, wind down the windows and get seriously nostalgic, every time.

TELL US HOW YOUR PHOTOGRAPHY JOURNEY GOT STARTED? A few years ago, I picked up my mum's camera on a family holiday and started taking photos of people surfing – I just instantly fell in love with it. I'd scroll through Roxy and Rip Curl campaigns in my downtime and just mentally took myself to these dreamy locations. I thought to myself, 'I'll get there one day". >

Crank up the music, wind down the window.

DO YOU HIT THE ROAD MORE OFTEN SINCE BECOMING A PHOTOGRAPHER?

Definitely! The best trips are with my friends though, and taking photos for fun. We'll pull over on the side of the road and someone will do something ridiculous, and I'll snap a shot. It means the world to me to do trips with my friends because I'm away from home a lot, so I really appreciate how much they mean to me. They bring me back down to earth.

WHAT DOES THE OCEAN MEAN TO YOU?

It's my comfort and the only constant thing in my life. It's not going anywhere.

WHAT'S THE LONGEST TIME YOU'VE SPENT ON THE ROAD?

14 weeks, when my parents took me out of school. We packed up everything and just hit the road with a caravan. We headed west across the Nullarbor to Perth, then all the way up to Broome, across through the Northern Territory, over to Cairns and then all the way back home. I loved the landscape from Perth all the way to Broome. That was amazing! I really want to do that again, it's so barren and there's nothing there, but it's still so beautiful.

YOU'VE BEEN ON SOME EPIC TRIPS - WHAT'S THE BEST CAR YOU'VE ROAD TRIPPED IN?

Once in Bali, we drove this crazy light blue Volkswagen 181 convertible to a shoot. It was so nice driving home after a long day. We were all silent, had the music going and the wind blowing in our hair.

THE MOST BEAUTIFUL PLACE YOU'VE WOKEN UP IN?

On the beach in my hometown, Mount Martha! Over summer we had a bunch of us sleeping out under the stars at our local beach. My friends had a boat shed down there, so we made a fire, had some beers and just crashed. I had a towel, sleeping bag and made myself comfy in my little nook in the sand. Waking up on the beach was just amazing.

AND THE WILDEST PLACE YOU'VE SLEPT?

On an overnight bus going through some dodgy parts of Vietnam.

MOST BEAUTIFUL ROAD YOU'VE DRIVEN?

Great Ocean Road in Victoria. It gets me every time. Snaking in and around where the ocean meets the coast - it's amazing!

ANY SECRET SECLUDED SPOTS YOU CAN SHARE WITH US?

There's a rad dirt track out the back of Crescent Head, in New South Wales, where there are some great surf spots. We would jump in the back and try and find waves right along there.

THE FEELING YOU GET WHEN BEING ON THE ROAD?

Very nostalgic. I've kinda recently just discovered that I get the most inspired when I'm staring out a window, thinking, listening to inspiring music and just reflecting on things. When I am in the car, I like when the music starts playing - we all stop talking and just zen out.

COMFORT OR ADVENTURE? I like a balance of both. I'm willing to sacrifice comfort for adventure though.

MUST-HAVE ITEMS YOU BRING ON A ROAD TRIP? Music, swimsuit, camera.

TIPS FOR LIFE ON THE ROAD? Make sure you don't spend the whole time on your phone. Lift your head and take in your surroundings. It makes me sad when sometimes I'll look back in the car and someone's on their phone while we're going past an insane monument or area.

BEST TIPS TO GET STUNNING TRAVEL PICS? Break the rules. If you see a spot you want to get to that you think will make a really good photo, then go for it. With travel, try and include as many aspects as you can. If you have a wider picture, that's what it's all about - seeing all the different elements of a place. Get as much as you can into it.

YOUR TIPS FOR PEOPLE WHO WANT YOUR LIFE? Work hard. And never ever give up. If you have a dream then go for it. I didn't want to settle for a job I didn't like. I'm spontaneous, I'm one of these people that would drop everything to go chase dreams, go see someone on the other side of the world if they needed me. If you want it, just go for it.

A ROAD TRIP YOU'RE DREAMING OF GOING ON? Across the United States, LA to NYC.

YOUR LIFE MISSION? To live life with a purpose. A happy purpose.

WHAT'S NEXT FOR CAIT MIERS? I'm heading to California for a few weeks, then going to meet up with my brother and best friends in Central America for about 5 months. ♥

See Cait on Instagram @caitmiersphotography

cait miers

THE PEOPLE.

THE ADVENTURES.

№ 3

THREE

FROM

TO

START DATE

END DATE

Let's road trip...

THIS ROAD TRIP BEGAN WHEN

THE GOAL IS

PLANNED STOPS

I CHOSE THIS ADVENTURE BECAUSE

I'M IMAGINING IT WILL BE

I'M MOST LOOKING FORWARD TO

WE'LL BE DRIVING IN A

IT WAS CHOSEN BECAUSE

IF MONEY WAS NO OPTION, I WOULD HAVE TRAVELLED IN A

MY TRAVEL BUDDIES ARE

HOW I MET THEM

BUCKET LIST ITEMS I'M HOPING TO TICK OFF ALONG THE WAY

Wake up early and watch the sunrise. There's something magnificent about watching a day break. A magic moment that doesn't cost a thing.

Date:
Place:

TODAY IS DAY   OF THE ROAD TRIP

I WOKE UP IN

THE WEATHER WAS

WE DECIDED TO STOP HERE BECAUSE

THE BEST THING I ATE

THE MOST INTERESTING PERSON I MET

I DISCOVERED

I LEARNED

CURRENT MOOD

A LITTLE SOMETHING ABOUT EACH OF MY TRAVEL BUDDIES

OUR ADVENTURES TOGETHER

ON OUR TO-DO LIST

COMPLETED

Y ☐ N ☐

Y ☐ N ☐

Y ☐ N ☐

Y ☐ N ☐

Y ☐ N ☐

Y ☐ N ☐

Being on the road makes me...

Feel

Dream about

Consider

Miss

Plan for

Excited about

the road is life

—Jack Kerouac

Date:

Place:

RIGHT NOW IT'S DAY   OF THE TRIP

I'M CURRENTLY

WE WANTED TO TRAVEL HERE BECAUSE

THE FIRST THING I DID HERE

THE PEOPLE ARE

I FEEL GRATEFUL FOR

THE LAST CONVERSATION I HAD

BEST MOMENT OF TODAY

HIDDEN GEM WE FOUND

I'M LOOKING FORWARD TO

WE TRAVELLED   KMS / MILES TODAY

TOMORROW WE WILL

PLACES WE'VE EXPLORED SO FAR

Practice an
accent in the car
and use it at the
next gas stop.

THE NEXT STOP IS

Date:
Place:

ROAD SIGN

ENCOUNTER

THING I SAW

MEAL I HAD

UNPLANNED STOP

STORY I HEARD

PERSON I THOUGHT ABOUT

I'LL NEVER FORGET...

let's run away together

Date:

Place:

TODAY WE ARRIVED IN

IT TOOK US _____ HRS AND _____ STOPS TO GET HERE FROM _____

WE WERE INSPIRED TO COME HERE BECAUSE

THE WILDEST MOMENT ALONG THE WAY

THE MOST PICTURESQUE SPOTS

A BEAUTIFUL ENCOUNTER

I'M DREAMING OF LIVING *(make it happen!)*

ADVENTURES I WANT TO HAVE TOMORROW

ADVENTURES WE HAD TODAY

I FELL ASLEEP IN

A TIME WE GOT INTO TROUBLE

SOMETHING I WISH I HAD PACKED

SOMETHING I PACKED AND NEVER USED

THINGS I'VE COLLECTED ALONG THE WAY

Lookin' back...

THE MOST MAGICAL MOMENT OF THE TRIP

MY FAVOURITE LOCATION

I WISH WE SPENT MORE TIME IN

THE PLACE I WOULD MOST LIKELY LIVE

THE MOST SPONTANEOUS THING I DID

A HIDDEN SECRET WE FOUND

THE FUNNIEST MEMORY

THE MOST INTERESTING PERSON I MET

THE MOST TRYING MOMENT

THIS TRIP MADE ME APPRECIATE

SOMETHING I LEARNED ABOUT MYSELF

I CAN'T GET THIS OUT OF MY HEAD

TASTIEST MEAL

TUNE OF THE TRIP

BEAUTIFUL SUNRISE

PRETTIEST SUNSET

BIGGEST HIGH

COZIEST NIGHT

BEST BED

ON MY NEXT ROAD TRIP I WANT TO

NOW AT THE END OF THE TRIP, I FEEL

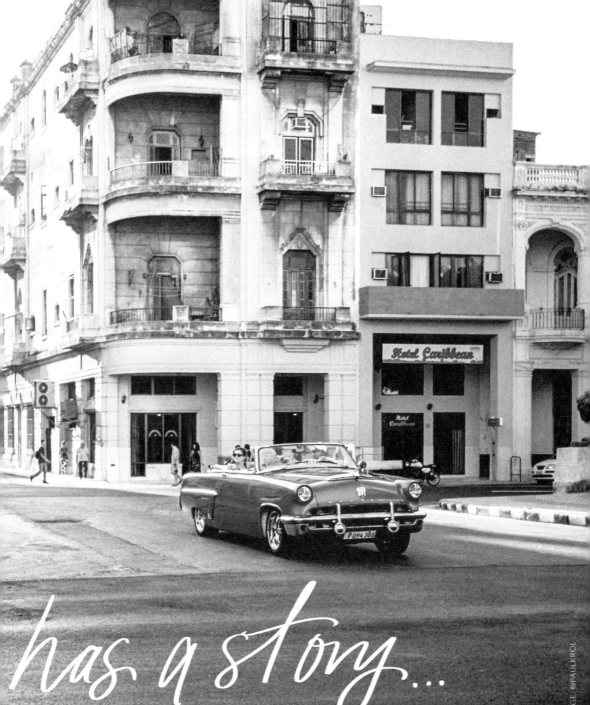

has a story...

snaphappy

Nº 3

Nº 3

Nº 3

FOUR

FROM

TO

START DATE

END DATE

Baby, let's drive...

THIS TIME I'M OFF TO

I'M EXCITED ABOUT

CREATORS OF THIS ROAD TRIP

FRIENDS COMING ALONG FOR THE RIDE

IT'S BEEN PLANNED SINCE

THE AMOUNT OF TIME WE HAVE

5 PLACES WE WANT TO SEE

LAST MINUTE THINGS TO ORGANISE

THE ANTICIPATION

Lost in the thrill of it all.

-Frank Ocean

THE WHEELS

OWNED BY

ODOMETER READING AT THE START OF THE TRIP

THREE WORDS THAT DESCRIBE IT

SKILLS I'M CONTRIBUTING TO THE JOURNEY

 AND MY TRAVEL BUDDIES' BEST SKILLS ARE

SOMETHING NO ONE KNOWS ABOUT ME

Who's who?

DJ

SNACK SUPPLIER

DRIVER

ADVENTURE PLANNER

N° 4

snap happy

THE FIRST DAYS

Date:

Place:

TODON IS   WHICH IS DAY   OF THE TRIP

I WOKE UP IN

WHICH WAS

WE ARE STAYING HERE FOR

TODAY'S PLANS

I WAS ENTERTAINED BY

I AMAZED MYSELF WHEN

IN THE EVENING WE

this place...

LOOKS

SOUNDS

FEELS

REMINDS ME OF

SMELLS

I HAD THE BEST TIME WHEN

TASTES

NEXT ON THE ITINERARY

When in the car...

I'M ENJOYING

I'M MISSING

I'M SMILING

I'M EATING

I'M DRINKING

I'M WEARING

I'M READING

I'M TEXTING

I'M REALISING

I'M LOVING

I CAN'T STOP SINGING

Date:

Place:

TODY IS DAY   OF THE TRIP

WE'RE CURRENTLY

THE BEST MOMENT SO FAR

FUNNIEST THING SAID IN THE CAR

BEST CREATION

A STORY I HEARD

I'M LOVING THIS TRIP BECAUSE

MY DAY WAS SPENT

THE BEST NIGHT HAS BEEN

MY LAST KISS *(where, when, who, how?)*

An article, a story or an interesting fact.... read something out loud to your road trip partner.

the sky's the limit...

WHAT WOULD YOU DO IF YOU KNEW YOU COULDN'T FAIL?

IF YOU COULD BECOME A MASTER AT ANYTHING, WHAT WOULD YOU CHOOSE?

WHAT'S YOUR WILDEST DREAM?

IMAGINE THAT YOU COULD LIVE A DAY WITHOUT CONSEQUENCES... WHAT WOULD YOU DO?

WHAT EPIC ADVENTURE ARE YOU DREAMING OF NEXT?

IF YOU COULD TIME TRAVEL, WHAT YEAR WOULD YOU GO TO?

IF YOU COULD HAVE A SUPERPOWER FOR ONE DAY, WHICH POWER WOULD YOU CHOOSE?

IF YOU COULD CHANGE ONE THING IN THIS WORLD, WHAT WOULD IT BE?

Write a letter to your future self

WHAT ADVICE WOULD YOU GIVE YOUR YOUNGER SELF?

All I really want to do
is spend my life travelling
the world, sitting on rocks,
looking at views that take
my breath away, drinking tea
on different balconies, dancing
to good music, road-tripping
on weekends, and lying beneath
blankets of stars.
Is that really too much
to ask for?

MOLLIE BYLETT

Date:
Place:

RIGHT NOW WE'RE IN

LAST NIGHT WE SLEPT IN

NATURE WE'VE EXPLORED

ANIMALS WE'VE SPOTTED

FRESH PRODUCE WE'VE FOUND

YUMMIEST MEAL WE'VE MADE

ROADS WE'VE TRAVELLED

I PROCRASTINATED WHEN

PLACES I'VE SHOWERED

TREATS I'VE ENJOYED

THINGS I'VE GOOGLED

ITEMS I'VE COLLECTED ON THE WAY

PEOPLE I HAVE A CRUSH ON

TRAITS I LOVE ABOUT MY TRAVEL BUDDIES

QUESTIONS I WANT ANSWERED

MOMENTS I WON'T FORGET FROM THIS TRIP

the highlights...

TEENY TINY PLACES WE FOUND

I TRIED THIS FOR THE FIRST TIME

INCREDIBLE PEOPLE I MET

PLACES I FELL IN LOVE WITH

NIGHTS OUT (*or in*)

VIEWS THAT BLEW MY MIND

BEST MOMENT IN THE CAR

FUNNIEST STORY FROM THE SCAVENGER HUNT

the best...

BED

SLEEP

EAT

DRINK

SUNRISE

SUNSET

SINGER

DRIVER

TUNE

SURPRISE

QUOTE OF THE TRIP

ROAD TRIP ITEM TICKED OFF

MOMENTS
I loved on this trip

Nº 4

N° 4

Smile at every
stranger you
cross paths
with today.

LIFE *in the* SLOW*lane*

Marlow

Quin

Courtney

Ivy

Michael

Easton

"Let's sell the house and travel around the world for a year" - was something bohemian-spirited Courtney Adamo asked her husband almost every night for twelve years. She couldn't believe it when one day he finally said yes - and life has never been the same since.

It all began with Courtney's childhood dream and longing to explore the world on the road with her family, one country at a time. Living in London with successful careers (Michael, a Managing Director of his production company and Courtney, a founder of family lifestyle website *Babyccino Kids*), they decided to leave the predictability of normal life and embark on a dream journey to find a place they like to call 'somewhere slower'.

It was New Year's Day 2015 when the couple put their dream into action, and sat the kids down to explain they'd be leaving everything behind to explore the world together for a year. With only one concern from their eldest son, Easton, 'who's going to water my lemon tree?', they were all ready to go.

Michael and Courtney then did what some called crazy; they sold their newly renovated home and all of their material belongings to finance their year of travel, took the kids out of school, put their careers on hold, and hit the road for what was to become an adventure of a lifetime.

Fast forward six months into their journey, the family has ventured from London to the USA, South America, New Zealand, Australia, Japan and Sri Lanka. With Portugal and Italy left to tick off on their incredible year-long adventure, the Adamos have enjoyed invaluable moments together, opened their children up to the world around them, and fulfilled their dream of finding a slower pace of life.

WHERE DID THE IDEA TO PACK IT ALL UP AND LIVE ON THE ROAD COME FROM?

Courtney - It's been a dream of mine since I was very young. I grew up on a tulip farm in rural Washington State and my grandparent's neighbours did exactly that. They took their children out of school, put their careers on hold and travelled the world. It was a daring move for a family in small-town America and everyone was intrigued, including my eight-year-old self.

MICHAEL, IT TOOK 12 YEARS TO CONVINCE YOU TO GO. HOW DO YOU FEEL ABOUT YOUR DECISION NOW? Ahh amazing, I'm so glad we did it. It was the best decision we made! We can't complain about our life in London, we had a really nice lifestyle and I was very comfortable in it - but Courtney kept pushing and I am so glad she did.

WHAT SPARKED YOU TO FINALLY GO?

We wanted to have more one-on-one time with our kids while they are still young. They grow up really quickly, and we were shocked when Easton turned ten - there's something about going into double digits that's a real milestone for parents. We really wanted to slow down and appreciate our time together, and we really wanted to introduce the kids to different cultures of the world and show them different ways of living. It just felt like the right time to step out of the rat race and be on the sidelines.

COURTNEY, YOU'RE THE FOUNDER OF BABYCCINO KIDS, ARE YOU STILL WORKING ON THAT? Yeah - I work around 4-5 hours a day, fitting it around what we're doing. Michael isn't working on the road, so he is doing all the home schooling when I work.

SO PRINCIPAL ADAMO, HOW HAVE YOU FOUND HOME SCHOOLING THE KIDS? To teach your own children isn't very easy. I had to learn how to be a teacher - I didn't really know how to do it. If you don't know what you're talking about, the kids know instantly, so you have to come prepared. I learned that the hard way! We try and study every weekday, if we miss a day, we make up for it on the weekend. Or, if we do something really interesting one day, like a walking trip through Kyoto - that counts as a lesson. I have so much respect for teachers now and how they do this with thirty kids in a room. >

let's go somewhere slow...

51.5074° N / 0.1278° W

NOW THAT YOU'VE EXPERIENCED LIFE ON THE ROAD AS A FAMILY, WHAT DO YOU THINK LIFE WILL BE LIKE WHEN YOU RETURN? *Michael* - Life will be different for sure. We will really resist falling into the rat race again. Even though we had a nice life in London, it's a constant treadmill. You're always running to keep up - and when you're on it, you don't even realise it. The people around you are all working long hours, striving for bigger salaries and wanting bigger and better and faster. Your reality gets so skewed, and you start placing importance on things that really aren't important. It's funny how just stepping off of that treadmill allows you to see what really matters. Many things that used to matter to us, seem silly or trivial now.

TELL US ABOUT ONE OF YOUR FAVOURITE ROAD TRIPS? *Courtney* - We loved driving Route 66 through the desert to Joshua Tree - it was so crazy beautiful. We also went from Los Angeles up the coast of California to Santa Cruz, and then cut inland to Yosemite, which was beautiful and dramatic. When you drive out on the eastern side of Yosemite, it's completely different to how it looked when you came in. That is the amazing thing about America - you can drive for an hour and it's like you've gone to another planet.

ANY WILD ENCOUNTERS ON THE ROAD? *Courtney* - We drove across Sri Lanka and were warned about the danger of elephants on the road. In the final half hour of our drive, in total darkness, we came upon a massive bull elephant in front of us. We quickly turned the car off, killed the headlights, quieted the kids and sat motionless so he wouldn't feel provoked. As the giant male strode within inches of our van, the kids thought it was the most incredible thing they've ever seen!

THE MOST IDYLLIC VILLAGE? *Courtney* - We think Trancoso in Brazil is one of the most magical places we've ever been.

WHAT ARE SOME 'FIRSTS' YOU'VE DONE LATELY? *Courtney* - Surfing with dolphins! We weren't intending to camp in Porpoise Bay, New Zealand, but we made a last-minute decision to stay there despite foul weather. The next morning we awoke to sunshine for the first time in seven days, and surfed with Hector dolphins all day long. They were just so playful – jumping around the kids and surfing the waves with them. It was a day they'll never forget.

A CULTURAL ASPECT THE KIDS LOVED? *Courtney* - The girls loved wearing their yukatas (kimonos) in Japan, and didn't want to take them off. In the end, we had to buy two to take home with us.

WHAT MAKES YOU SMILE? *Michael* - Simply watching the kids. Watching them enjoy the adventure and discovering our amazing world along the way. Little Marlow, for example, would say 'konichiwa' to total strangers on the street in Japan - that made me and the strangers smile.

A PHRASE YOU OVERUSE IN THE FAMILY? *Courtney* - 'Don't forget your shoes!'

WHAT DO YOU LOVE MOST ABOUT BEING ON THE ROAD? *Courtney* - The freedom of being able to go wherever you want to go, whenever you want to go. In a campervan, you have everything you need. Everywhere you go, your home is with you.

LIVING ON THE ROAD FULL-TIME WITH FOUR KIDS MUST BE DIFFICULT AT TIMES? *Courtney* - There are some trying moments. When we were in New Zealand, it rained for fifteen days straight and we were stuck inside a campervan. But I still loved it - we had wet clothes, everything smelled, we had four kids in a small space and I was still like 'whatever, I've got all I need right now.'

WHAT IS YOUR TRAVEL ADVICE FOR ROAD TRIPPING FAMILIES?

Courtney - Just do it - don't over think it. *Michael* - Pack what you think you need. Then take away half of it - you don't need it!

FAVOURITE DISCOVERY?

Courtney - Chai tea from a thermos served after surfing in the frigid ocean off Chile.

ALL TIME FAVOURITE ROAD TRIP DISH?

Courtney - Our 'Pasta Alla Campervan', a recipe we've modified from a classic Italian dish. It's basically tuna, olives, capers and tomato sauce over penne pasta. The kids go crazy for it!

WOULD YOU DO IT ALL OVER AGAIN?

Both - YES! We'd happily keep going for another year!

WHAT'S NEXT FOR THE ADAMO FAMILY?

Courtney - This year has really changed us and I don't think we'll ever live the same – we'll opt for somewhere slower. We've fallen in love with almost every place we've been so it's going to be hard to decide. We didn't go to South America thinking we'd ever live there, but we could easily settle in Brazil, Uruguay or Chile. We've also checked out the coast of California, and parts of Australia and New Zealand as places we'd like to live. One place that really captured our hearts though is Byron Bay in Australia. We'd love to move there and set up a family business. Stay tuned! ♥

See the Adamo's on Instagram @courtneyadamo

the adamo family

ONE
motto we live by

"Piano, piano"
(Italian for slowly, slowly)

TWO
favourite restaurants in the world

Da Vincenzo - Positano, Italy
& La Huella - Jose Ignacio, Uruguay

THREE
words to describe the Adamo's

Adventurous, appreciative, vivacious
- we're not the quietest group!

FOUR
amazing places you discovered

Waipatiki, NZ Puertochillo, Chile.
Espehlo Beach, Brazil. Arugam Bay,
Sri Lanka.

FIVE
items picked up along the way

Feathers, friendship bracelets, poncho's,
coconut palm hats & surfboards

N° 5

FIVE

FROM

TO

START DATE

END DATE

Date:

Place:

It's road trip time again!

THIS TIME I AM CRUISING WITH

THE FIRST STRETCH OF ROAD WE'RE HITTING

FINAL DESTINATION

WE HAVE   DAYS / HOURS TO GET THERE

WE WILL BE ...

A) CRUISING LIKE A CONVERTIBLE

B) STOPPING EVERYWHERE AND ANYWHERE LIKE A CURIOUS KOMBI

C) ON A MISSION, STOPPING ONLY WHERE WE NEED TO... 007 STYLE IN AN ASTON MARTIN

OUR RIDE LOOKS LIKE

THE SPOTS WE CAN'T MISS OUT ON

OUR FIRST DAY *(and the mischief we got up to)*

Date:

Place:

TODAY IS _____ WHICH IS DAY _____ OF THE TRIP

THE MORNING WAS SPENT _____

_____

_____

_____

I'M WEARING _____

_____

I'M STRUGGLING WITH _____

_____

I'M LOVING ABOUT LIFE RIGHT NOW _____

_____

_____

_____

THE BIGGEST THINGS I'M THINKING ABOUT _____

_____

_____

_____

Nº 5

TODAY'S PLANS

WHAT WE ACTUALLY DID

explore the world

CLEAR

with eyes wide open

IN THE CAR

Who is the...

FUNNIEST?

WORST NAVIGATOR?

BEST AT MAKING FRIENDS?

CRAZIEST DRIVER?

BIGGEST CHATTERBOX?

MOST LIKELY TO GET A FINE?

MOST LIKELY TO BE HANGRY? *(and how we solve this)*

SNACKS WE KEEP MUNCHING ON

OUR KILLER PLAYLIST

RANDOM CAR CHATS

THE LAST 24 HOURS

Date:

Place:

IT'S NOW DAY   OF THE ROAD TRIP

MY DESCRIPTION OF THIS PLACE

POPULATION

THE PLAN IS

CULTURAL ASPECTS I FOUND FASCINATING

I CAN'T WAIT TO

TONIGHT WE'RE CRASHING AT

THE SPOTS WE'VE EXPLORED...

the journey so far...

snap happy

THE ADVENTURE

THE JOURNEY.

Date:

Place:

THE LAST   DAYS IN WORDS

PEOPLE I'VE GOTTEN TO KNOW

SOME INTERESTING FACTS

Catch...

A SECOND

AN HOUR

A MINUTE

A MORNING

AN AFTERNOON

A NIGHT

A DAY

WHEN TIME STOOD STILL

Summin' up my road trip...

A PLACE I FELL IN LOVE WITH

I WAS OVER-THE-MOON HAPPY WHEN

THE MOST UNUSUAL PLACE I FOUND MYSELF

A MOMENT WHEN I COULDN'T STOP LAUGHING

BEST TOWNS WE VISITED

MOST RANDOM STOP

SCARIEST MOMENT

CLOTHES I WORE ON REPEAT

CAFE I WANT TO BRING BACK HOME

NEW WORDS I LEARNED

Nº 5

CRAZIEST DAY

QUIRKIEST PERSON

A HIGH

A LOW

GREATEST ADVENTURE

A GORGEOUS DAY

A GREAT NIGHT

LONGEST DRIVE

BEST ROAD

IT WAS PICTURE PERFECT WHEN

N° 5

life on the road

"We lived everyday like it was our last. We weren't money hungry, so if we had enough money to live, we'd go and see beautiful things. I remember when my parents heard about a random hot spring in the middle of nowhere that was like a thousand miles away. We just left what we were doing and went - it was a wonderful life like that". - Orion Griffiths.

With a car as his home and Europe as his playground, every day was an exciting new adventure for Orion Griffiths growing up on the road. From humble beginnings as a busker to the bright lights of Broadway, this multi-talented street performer was born into a world like no other - a travelling family circus.

From the moment you meet Orion, you're instantly drawn in by his charming British accent and beautiful, positive energy. This incredible 28 year old has road tripped his entire life, making thousands of people smile along the way.

Named after the constellation, *Orion's Belt*, Orion has really lived up to his name and become a star. It all began before he was even born, when his musical parents decided to live a life less ordinary. They refused to be tied down to the system and wanted their kids to grow up free - so they hit the road and formed The Sardine Family Circus.

The second youngest of eight children, Orion travelled the streets performing acrobatic tricks with his siblings, while his mum juggled and his dad played the guitar. They slept, ate, studied, trained and performed on the road while roaming from country to country, sharing their talents and living each day like it was their last. The family never valued money or possessions, they earned enough to be happy and simply lived for the love of performing and being free.

Orion was 24 when he finally settled down in Los Angeles to pursue his dream of acting, and for the first time lived what he calls a 'normal life' in one place. A legend in the circus world and the star of every stage he's graced since, it wasn't long before he was casting for roles in Hollywood and was headhunted for the Broadway musical, *Pippin*.

Now based in San Francisco running a circus school and sharing his passion, Orion has his sights set on competing in the International Monte Carlo Circus Festival, venturing to the Himalayas, and chasing his dream of starring in a major motion picture. With performing in his blood and travelling in his soul, the sky's the limit for this rising star!

ORION VENTURE MAXIMILIAN FITZ GRIFFITHS - YOU'RE A MAN WITH FIVE NAMES! TELL US WHERE THEY CAME FROM.

Orion: Mum and Dad were doing a show in Holland, where it is very muggy, wet and cloudy. My mum had most of us kids in the back of the car, but when I was born, she wanted to go to the hospital. My parents tried to leave after my birth, but they weren't allowed to leave without naming me; they had to get it onto the birth certificate. When dad walked outside to calm down, he looked up at the sky, which had cleared, and saw Orion's belt.

Venture: When you grow up on the road, you move a lot and you adapt quickly. Mum always really wanted to call one of her kids 'Venture' because of that.

Maximilian: Dad, just wanting to call one of his kids 'Maximilian'!

Fitz: After my grandma.

HOW DID THE FAMILY CIRCUS START?

While travelling through the Ukraine, my parents pulled up for the night next to a convoy of seven cars, which turned out to be a travelling circus. As fate would have it, the circus's guitarist had been injured and couldn't perform. My dad happened to be a guitarist and offered to help. Working with the circus meant that my older siblings played with the circus kids all day, and slowly started to learn their tricks. Before they knew it, we had started a little family circus, going by the nickname of 'The Sardines' - because of the way our family looked piling out of the car!

WHAT WAS THE FIRST TRICK YOU LEARNED?

I was two and a half when I learned the Chinese yo-yo. My mum came out and was like, "you're doing it!". I then took a liking to acrobatics, I remember watching it and thinking, "this is what I want to do." >

DO YOU HAVE A SPECIALTY? My favourite trick at the moment is hand balancing on one arm. It's one of the harder things to accomplish - it's a patience game. I've incorporated it in my Rolla Bolla act, where you balance on five different cylinders on different angles. There are very few people who can do this move - I'm still perfecting it.

YOUR CAR WAS LITERALLY YOUR HOME. YOU ALL LIVED IN THERE? Yeah, we travelled in a Bedford CA for a long time before mum and dad got a Mercedes 508. We travelled in it for ten years and put over a 1,000,000 miles on it before we sold it again!

YOU WERE CONSTANTLY MOVING - HOW DID YOU DECIDE WHERE TO GO? My parents were living in the moment, going where they wanted. We would follow the heat. If it was cold and snowing, we would go work in warmer places like Italy or Rome. We street performed as a family around the entire world, going from city to city, always finding towns to perform in. We would build a huge crowd in a foreign country in the middle of nowhere, just to get enough money to move on to the next place.

DID YOU GO TO SCHOOL? We were home schooled - by my dad mainly. Maybe I'm not as well educated and I have no shame in saying that. I might not be the best at reading or writing and putting pen to paper, but you can drop me off anywhere in the world and I will survive. I received a lot of common sense and unconditional love from my mum and dad, that's all I could ask for.

WERE YOU EVER JEALOUS OF NORMAL LIFE? Oh yes, I'm not going to lie to you - of course I was. I would see kids with Play Stations, they would have Xboxes and have their own bedroom. I remember those kids saying to me, "dude you have the coolest life". When you grow up with nothing, it makes you appreciate everything and I wouldn't change it for the world.

TELL US ABOUT THE BEST THINGS ABOUT LIFE ON THE ROAD? Well, you don't have to pay rent, you always meet new people and make new friends and you're able to have any garden you want! Having everything so close to you is great too, you can do everything immediately and when you're done driving you can crawl over the seat to bed. On the road, there are times of clarity. There are moments of nothingness. There are moments of perfection. That's what we spend most of our lives looking for.

WHAT DID MEAL TIME LOOK LIKE FOR YOUR FAMILY ON THE ROAD? We were so poor growing up, we weren't able to eat that lavishly - we ate at a very basic level. But we ended up eating lots of fruit and vegetables because we would go to the local markets and find the best deals.

WHAT WAS YOUR FAVOURITE CULTURAL ASPECT? In Morocco, dinner is a very special time and the people all eat off of the same plate. It really shocked me how close they are. They all sit down around the food, sharing spoons and talking about what's happening in their lives.

TELL US ABOUT A MEMORABLE ROAD TRIP? I remember being blown away by how big America was when we arrived. We went on a three month road trip from Key West in Florida to San Francisco, driving slowly down south through Louisiana and stopping along the way to find towns to perform in. Man, did we get to see what America was like on that trip! It was unbelievable.

WHEN DID YOU HEAD OFF ON YOUR OWN?
I left the family circus in 2013 and went to Broadway after being cast in the musical, *Pippin*. I remember watching the movie 'Terminator' when I was a kid and saying I wanted to be an actor - I was dreaming of that since I was eight, and started chasing that dream.

WHO IS THE MOST INSPIRING PERSON YOU'VE MET ALONG THE WAY?
My sister. At just nine years old, she was electrocuted while we were in Austria for a performance. She was in a coma, lost an arm and suffered scarring to 90% of her body. Despite having everything taken away so young, she is still so positive. She is what inspires me to be the best I can be, not only for me but for her - to do some of the stuff she never got to do.

WHAT'S YOUR FAVOURITE SNACK ON THE ROAD?
A peanut butter sandwich - it's just everything! We're British right, so we drink four or five cups of tea a day. I would take my peanut butter sandwich and dip it in my tea and when I am eating that, I am living life to the fullest!

THE MOST UNUSUAL PLACE YOU'VE SLEPT?
It was in the Granada Mountains in Spain - I slept in the natural hot springs all night! I woke up at 5am and realised I slept through, my body was just so relaxed and switched off.

THE MOST BEAUTIFUL STRETCH OF ROAD?
I remember driving through Italy, going along a winding road around Mount Pellegrino - some of that stretch is ridiculous, it's like a painting.

WHAT TRAVEL ADVICE DO YOU HAVE FOR OTHER ROAD TRIPPERS?
Don't ever park in a rest stop! Drive twenty more miles and you're going to find a river where there is flowing water, birds

orion griffiths

moving - you're going to find paradise. Don't ever settle for a rest stop, that's the world pushing you where they want you to go.

WHAT DOES LIFE ON THE ROAD MEAN TO YOU?
When you first learn how to walk, you have to fall - because that's what walking is, it's falling. Living on the road is falling, but each time you fall - you catch yourself. That's what life on the road is to me. You don't know what's in front of you, but you have to take that fall to find out. ❤

See Orion on Instagram @orion_griffiths

SIX

FROM

TO

START DATE

END DATE

BEFORE...

IN   DAYS / WEEKS I AM OFF ON AN ADVENTURE TO

THE PEOPLE JOINING ME ARE

WE'VE BEEN ORGANIZING IT SINCE
THE IDEA CAME FROM

I CAN'T WAIT TO

WE NEED TO DECIDE ON

WE HEREBY NAME THIS TRIP

PLACES WE'VE BEEN RECOMMENDED TO CHECK OUT

TOTAL BUDGET

FOOD

GAS

ACCOMMODATION

SPENDING MONEY

Draw the planned route...

Date:
Place:

RIGHT NOW, IT'S THE END OF DAY   OF THE ROAD TRIP

WE WOKE UP IN   AT   AM / PM AND WENT TO EXPLORE

I WAS WEARING

WE HAD BREAKFAST AT

I ATE

MY DAY HAS BEEN

I WAS ENTERTAINED BY

WE VISITED

I COULDN'T STOP

ON THE ROAD WE

I REALLY ENJOYED

THE BEST THING ABOUT BEING ON THE ROAD

YET, I DO MISS

MY BED FOR THE NIGHT LOOKS LIKE

RIGHT NOW, I'M ABOUT TO

Explore an old
building - go
to every floor
and every room
if you can.

ON THE ROAD

MOST FREQUENT DRIVER

BACKSEAT DRIVING COMMENTS

SNACKS WE EAT

SONGS WE SING

CHATS WE HAVE

OUT THE WINDOW WE SEE

THINGS WE LAUGH AT

A TEMPER LOST

THE MESSIEST PERSON

REASONS WE STOP

SECRETS REVEALED

TIMES WE GOT LOST *(whose fault?)*

Let's **FIND SOME BEAUTIFUL PLACE TO GET LOST.**

Date:

Place:

WE'VE BEEN ON THE ROAD FOR _____ DAYS NOW

I CAN'T REMEMBER THE LAST TIME I _____

YESTERDAY I LOVED _____

_____

_____

_____

TODAY WAS FUN BECAUSE _____

_____

_____

_____

I WOULD DESCRIBE THIS TRIP AS _____

_____

_____

_____

MY STAPLE FOOD

GO-TO OUTFIT

WORDS WE OVERUSE

TUNE ON REPEAT

HILARIOUS THINGS WE'VE SAID

SOUNDTRACK OF THE TRIP

A LITTLE SOMETHING ABOUT THE PEOPLE I'M WITH

THE CAR IS CURRENTLY   SPOTLESS / COULD DO WITH A CLEAN / A MESS / A HOARDER'S HOME

a page for a friend
to insert their story

MY NAME IS

I'M CURRENTLY IN

I'M HERE TO

I GREW UP IN

NOW I LIVE

YOU & I MET *(when, where, how)*

MY FIRST IMPRESSION OF YOU WAS

TOGETHER WE HAVE

I LOVE THAT YOU

THE WEIRDEST THING ABOUT YOU

Nº 6

MY FUNNIEST MEMORY WITH YOU

I WILL ALWAYS THINK ABOUT YOU WHEN

YOU'VE TAUGHT ME

I'VE TAUGHT YOU

A SONG THAT REMINDS ME OF YOU

IN FIVE YEARS, I THINK YOU'LL BE

AND I'LL BE

MY ADVICE FOR YOU

D&M *(deep and meaningful)* CONVERSATIONS

Date:

Place:

IT'S DAY _____ . WE'VE DRIVEN _____ KMS / MILES

THIS MORNING I WOKE UP IN _____

MY BED WAS _____

OUT THE WINDOW I SAW _____

THE FIRST THING I DID _____

MY TRIP HERE WAS _____

THE DAY CONSISTED OF _____

I'M FINDING THIS PLACE TO BE _____

A FUN MEMORY

A WILD MEMORY

A SCARY MEMORY

AN EMBARRASSING MEMORY

A SPECIAL MOMENT

I have no idea where this will lead us, but I have a definite feeling it will be a place both wonderful and strange – Special Agent Dale Cooper, Twin Peaks

On this trip, have you...

GONE SWIMMING

FOUND A NEW PASSION

HAD A LIGHTBULB MOMENT

MET AN INCREDIBLE PERSON

WATCHED THE SUNSET

GOTTEN LOST

FELT ALIVE

READ A BOOK

SUNG AT THE TOP OF YOUR LUNGS

TRIED SOMETHING NEW

MADE A NEW FRIEND

BROKEN THE LAW

FALLEN IN LOVE *(or broken a heart?)*

SUMMARY

THE GREATEST MORNING

BEST NIGHT

PLACES WE SLEPT

COSIEST BED

LONGEST DAY

ARGUMENTS IN THE CAR

WE COULDN'T STOP LAUGHING WHEN

LOUDEST PERSON IN THE CAR

MOST MEMORABLE MEAL

I'M SO HAPPY THAT

Put down your
phone for a day.
Turn it off and
just enjoy the
simplicity of life

Born to be wild

Meet model & insta-babe Mimi Elashiry, a bohemian, beach-born ballerina breaking boundaries, and taking the fashion world by storm

mimi elashiry

From the moment you're surrounded by her infectious energy, it's obvious that it's not just Mimi's unconventional height making her a standout in the fashion industry. Standing at just 5'6", this natural, free-spirited beauty is also a talented ballet dancer, a fashion designer and a photographer with a passion for vintage cameras.

Thanks to a huge global following on social media and her unique Australian-Egyptian background, Mimi is hot property in the modelling world. Signed to one of L.A.'s biggest agencies, she's been featured in *Teen Vogue*, has sparked the interests of huge labels like *Victoria's Secret* and *Calvin Klein*, and has also fronted major clothing labels *Diesel* and *Free People*. Her love for being on the road has also landed her the dream gig of hopping music festivals across the country with *MTV Australia*.

Yet, despite her rise to fame, Mimi is still a down-to-earth, carefree spirit who just goes with the flow. She's the type of gentle soul who goes to the dog park to play with stranger's dogs, a curious mind who pulls apart leaves for hours because she likes their intricacies, and despite her hectic schedule, still takes time to collect rocks, feathers and twigs wherever she wanders.

At her core, Mimi was born to be wild. When she's not in front of the camera, this fearless earth child doesn't care about being seen at glamorous industry parties. Instead, you'll find her hitting the road on grungy road trips into the middle of nowhere to get lost and soak up the beauty of Mother Nature.

YOUR UNCONVENTIONAL BREAKTHROUGH INTO THE MODELLING INDUSTRY IS VERY INSPIRING, TELL US HOW IT HAPPENED?

I started modelling when I was a child, I stopped when I was about eleven and never thought about it after that. School and ballet were my life really. When I got to high school, I would hang out around Bondi Beach and photographers started to approach me. They would send my test shots to agencies and then I'd go in to meet them and they would tell me, "you're too short". For a young girl it was a little heartbreaking, because they would constantly scout me and raise my hopes, only to reject me at castings. I've always loved photography, especially film photography, and I started to use Instagram as an outlet to show off my pictures - and it got people's attention. Then I started networking with people in the industry who introduced me to people, and it all just went from there.

TELL US MORE ABOUT YOUR LOVE FOR PHOTOGRAPHY?

I'm actually looking to move into doing more of it. I own five or six film cameras and always keep my Yashica T5 in my bag - I take it everywhere with me. I don't own a digital camera because I like to capture a moment instead of taking a million pictures of the same thing. With film, you capture a moment and can't edit it.

IF YOU WEREN'T A MODEL - WHAT WOULD YOU BE?

A dancer – one hundred percent! I got a scholarship at Reddam House in Australia so I could dance and still finish school. It was, and still is, my passion. When I was younger I dreamed to dance in one of Kanye West's short films. I appreciate how he works with ballerinas and contemporary dancers instead of just using girls in short shorts!

WE HEARD YOU'RE A BIT OF A CAMPER, WHERE DID THIS PASSION COME FROM?

I didn't really fit in at school. I'd go on road trips during the holidays to little festivals with some older friends. We'd camp for five or six days in the middle of nowhere – I'd sleep in a van. Camping trips became my outlet, and the source of my inspiration for all the creative writing I did during school. It made it a lot easier for me to come back and focus on dancing and studying.>

WHAT DO YOU LOVE MOST ABOUT IT? Just to be able to escape. As much as I appreciate everything in my life, I think escaping the concrete jungle and being in touch with the earth and surrounded by nature is so important. It's super grounding - I'm able to shut down, reset and really get in tune with my mind and body.

SUMMER, SPRING, AUTUMN OR WINTER? Spring, because the water is warm and all the flowers are blooming. I love flowers and I like to walk around and eat plants. When I was in Amsterdam last year there were begonia's everywhere - they are full of vitamin C and really crunchy!

YOU'VE HAD SOME AWESOME ROAD TRIPS! TELL US ABOUT SOME OF YOUR HIGHLIGHTS. I lived in Byron Bay last year, after three years of travelling the east coast of Australia. I would do road trips up to Noosa and the Sunshine Coast. I loved to surf and hang out, listen to music and sleep in the car. Being able to drive anywhere, move anywhere you want and wake up in the morning is just awesome.

I also did a motorbike trip into the desert on the back of a Harley. A group of us headed out for nine days - it was an amazing experience and I'll remember it for the rest of my life. We went from LA up through Nevada, onto Utah and then Arizona. We were blessed to stay with the Navajo Indians on their reservation. We stopped along the way, climbing up to lookouts and pitching our tents where we could see the sunrise. We would wake up at camp, and then ride for three to five hours to our next destination. It was unreal, but very challenging.

WHY WAS IT CHALLENGING? Riding a bike is like meditating - you're sitting on the back for hours just concentrating on the road. One day we drove for sixteen hours! It's amazing to just sit there and watch things go by, but you're forced to process and deal with your thoughts. I thought about some crazy stuff in my past that I had never tapped into. It was such an emotional journey for everyone. I think it was challenging to face myself like that - I'm always distracting myself at home with dancing or work. After that trip, I kind of realised that sitting and dealing with things is a very important thing to do.

WHAT WAS THE BEST PLACE YOU DISCOVERED? We found a hot spring in the middle of nowhere in freezing cold Utah. There was snow on the mountains around us and sheep everywhere. I had never been in a hot spring before… it was so surreal! We were so cold from riding the bikes so we sat there for like eight hours.

YOU HAVE AN EGYPTIAN BACKGROUND. HAVE YOU EVER ROAD TRIPPED THERE? Yeah, I went there eight years ago, when I was quite young and naive. We road tripped from Cairo to the Red Sea which was awesome - the huge sand dunes were amazing. I really want to go there again to appreciate it more.

DO YOU REMEMBER YOUR FIRST EVER ROAD TRIP? I road tripped to a small indie festival near Canberra called the 'Regrowth Festival'. Three or four thousand people gather in this beautiful green, mossy valley - they plant trees, listen to crazy music, paint pictures (and each other) and run wild, and free. We camped out in the car for 4 days - we strung fairy lights in it and looked up at the stars at night.

YOU SCORED A DREAM GIG WITH MTV AUSTRALIA COVERING FESTIVALS. WHAT IS IT ABOUT FESTIVALS THAT YOU LOVE? I love the crowds, I love being around people and feeding off all different kinds of energy, and I really love music. I love it when all sorts of people come together for the same reason - to have a good time and share it with their friends.

FAVE TRAVEL BUDDY My dog, Cha-cha. He's so chilled

WHAT'S ON YOUR ROAD TRIPPING PLAYLIST?
Tame Impala, Bob Moses, Sticky Fingers and Jonathan Wilson (my absolute favourite!)

YOU SEEM TO BE A TRUE ROAD TRIPPER AT HEART. COULD YOU BE ON THE ROAD FULL-TIME? Yes and no. I love being on the road – I crave that freedom. But, I'm also someone who needs to nest. I need somewhere I can create a sanctuary and have a place to keep my books – somewhere I can always come back to. Now that I travel for work, I really appreciate having a place to go back to and see the things I've collected on a shelf.

WHAT ROLE DO YOU USUALLY PLAY IN THE CAR?
I am a terrible navigator, let's be honest. I am usually the DJ and I feed the driver!

WHO WAS THE MOST MEMORABLE LOCAL YOU MET ALONG THE WAY? The Navajo Indians that we stayed with were so amazing.

ANY SECRET SPOTS YOU CAN SHARE WITH US? There's a secluded beach in Byron Bay called White's Beach. It's next to a mountain and covered in black volcanic rocks– you feel like you're in Hawaii. Not many people know about it and during the week it's usually empty.

3 WORDS YOU ASSOCIATE WITH LIFE ON THE ROAD? Freedom. Sunshine. Grounding.

HOW DOES LIFE ON THE ROAD FILL YOUR SOUL?
I think freedom is the most important aspect for me. It's good for the soul to let go of routine - as much as I love feeding off other people's energy and being in the city, I think it's really important to be able to escape that and have a reset in nature and with yourself. ♥

See Mimi on Instagram @mimielashiry

3 PEOPLE (DEAD OR ALIVE), YOU'D WANT TO ROAD TRIP WITH

A MOTTO YOU LIVE BY...

David Attenborough
Photographer, Annie Liebowitz
My boyfriend, Aden ♡

All you have is here & now.
So surrender & just be.

mimi elashiry

34.0522° N / 118.2437° W

THE PEOPLE.

THE ADVENTURES.

N⁰ 7

THE JOURNEY.

SEVEN

FROM

TO

START DATE

END DATE

Date:

Place:

I'M ON THE ROAD AND I'M FEELING

THE SEASON IS

I'M ROAD TRIPPING WITH

WE DECIDED TO DO THIS TRIP WHEN

THE HOT LITTLE WHEELS WE'RE DRIVING IN

COLOUR   YEAR

MODEL   OWNER

COMFINESS   CURRENT STATE

OTHER CARS CONVOYING WITH US

ESSENTIAL ITEMS I'VE PACKED   ...AND THE THINGS I FORGOT

PICTURE/DRAWING OF THE CAR

THE PLAN IS

ROAD TRIP CHECKLIST

☐
☐
☐
☐
☐
☐
☐
☐
☐
☐

Where I want to be in...

One week

One year

Three years

Ten years

Tomorrow

ALL THE CITIES I'VE BEEN TO IN THE WORLD   ...AND THE ONES I'D LOVE TO VISIT

Travelling is like flirting with life.
It's like saying, 'I would stay and love
you, but I have to go.'

- Lisa St Aubin de Teran

Date:
Place:

TODAY IS   WHICH IS DAY   OF THE ROAD TRIP

AN EMOTION THAT DESCRIBES ME RIGHT NOW

WE'RE CURRENTLY IN

I'M SMILING ABOUT

MY IMPRESSION OF THIS PLACE

I WILL REMEMBER IT FOR

FROM HERE, WE'RE GOING

DISTANCE WE'RE PLANNING TO COVER TODAY

TONIGHT WE'RE STOPPING AT

TONIGHT'S PLANS INCLUDE

N° 7

I'M HAPPY ABOUT

MY BIGGEST WORRY RIGHT NOW

MOMENTS I'LL NEVER FORGET

FACT OF THE DAY

Five minutes with a travel buddy...

YOUR FULL NAME

WHERE DO YOU CALL HOME

HOW DID YOU CELEBRATE YOUR LAST BIRTHDAY?

AND HOW MANY CANDLES WERE ON THE CAKE?

WHAT'S YOUR FIRST MEMORY OF ME?

WHAT ARE YOU DOING WHEN YOU'RE NOT ROAD TRIPPING?

THREE THINGS I DON'T KNOW ABOUT YOU

A MOTTO YOU LIVE BY

FIRST JOB YOU HAD

PROUDEST MOMENT

FIRST EVER ROAD TRIP

YOUR ALL-TIME FAVOURITE BAND

WHAT'S YOUR DREAM JOB

THE HIGHLIGHT OF THIS ROAD TRIP

YOUR FAVOURITE SPOT SO FAR

WHAT DO YOU LOVE ABOUT BEING ON THE ROAD?

BEST THING ABOUT ME AS A TRAVEL BUDDY

BUT, I ANNOY YOU WHEN

THREE PEOPLE, DEAD OR ALIVE, YOU WANT TO ROAD TRIP WITH AND WHY?

ONE OF THE BEST THINGS YOU'VE DONE IN YOUR LIFE

WHAT ARE YOU EXCITED ABOUT NEXT?

Date:

Place:

IT'S NOW DAY _____ OF THE ROAD TRIP

THINGS I DID TODAY

PEOPLE I SPOKE TO

RIGHT NOW I'M ABOUT TO

A STRANGE DREAM I RECENTLY HAD

What if you wake up one day and you're like 65, or 75, and you never got your novel or memoir written; or you didn't go swimming in the warm pools and oceans all those years because your thighs were jiggly and you had a nice big comfortable tummy; or you were just so strung out on perfectionism and people-pleasing that you forgot to have a big juicy creative life, of imagination and radical silliness and staring off into space like when you were a kid? It's going to break your heart. Don't let this happen.

— Anne Lamott

MISCHIEVIOUS
moments on the road

WE FOUND OURSELVES HERE BY MISTAKE

WE GOT IN A BIT OF A PICKLE WHEN

HOW WE GOT OUT OF IT

WHEN IT WENT WRONG

WHEN IT WENT OH-SO RIGHT!

...AND ALL THE OTHER CRAZINESS

Date:

Place:

TODAY IS DAY   OF THE ROAD TRIP AND WE'VE BEEN ON THE ROAD FOR   DAYS.

RIGHT NOW, I'M

THE PLAN FOR TODAY

I'M MOST EXCITED ABOUT

TONIGHT, WE'RE STAYING AT

ASK SOMEONE OLDER ABOUT A ROAD TRIP THEY WENT ON *(and what the world was like then)*

SUMMARY

FAVOURITE PLACE I WOKE UP IN

MOST AMAZING PLACE I FELL ASLEEP IN

THE BIGGEST DECISION

MOST EMBARRASSING THING I DID

TIMES WE GOT LOST

FUNNIEST QUOTES SAID IN THE CAR

A PERSONALITY I WON'T FORGET

BEST EXPERIENCE

MOST HILARIOUS MOMENT

THE BEST LOCALS I MET

MOST BREATHTAKING VIEW

A SERENDIPITOUS MOMENT

BEST ACCOMMODATION

WORST ACCOMMODATION

CAFES I ADORED

DESSERTS I TASTED

FAVOURITE TOURIST ATTRACTION

FAVOURITE PICTURE TAKEN

FAVOURITE PURCHASE

SONG OF THE TRIP

look for magic in the smallest things

My road trip...

Travelling Cars

A girl, her tiny toy cars, a camera and the open road.
Welcome to the world of Kim Leuenberger

Hey Kim! HEY AXEL & ASH! We're so in love with your quirky cars, tell us about the girl behind the lens? I'm a 24 year old Swiss girl living in London, never staying in one place, just ALWAYS ON THE GO somewhere. I'm kind of an old soul, but also a big kid at heart. Just happy to live really, and be close to nature. **How did you develop your love for toy cars?** As a teenager, I was obsessed with The Beach Boys and The Beatles… and just about ANYTHING FROM THE SIXTIES I was a bit of a hippie I guess! I would listen to all the music from Woodstock and would dream about owning one of those hippie vans. My parents saw these toy cars on a family holiday in Spain, one was blue had flowers on it - so they got it for me. It was like THE BEST GIFT EVER! **That's really cool! So where did the idea to take photos of them come from?** When Instagram first started, there was this project to raise awareness for World Autism Day. I wanted to help, so I took every toy I had on my shelf and started to take some pictures of them. My very first pic was this one of the van and Paddington Bear. I posted it on Instagram and the feedback was really good - people were commenting on how it made them smile and laugh. I was like, "that's nice feedback I WANT TO KEEP DOING THAT!" **So that's how the craze started?** Haha, kind of - I have so much fun taking these pictures - it's now been 5 years and I'm still doing it! IT'S JUST MY LITTLE ESCAPE… you know when you want to escape from reality, and just get into your little bubble. That's so easy for me! I just need to have my little toy cars and my camera and I'm gone for hours.

the small things ♡

51.5074° N / 0.1278° W

travelling cars

Where do you get these rad cars from? Oh - I have them spread out everywhere at people's houses! I mostly buy them in Spain, some in Italy and a few come from all over the place. I don't know really... there is just something about small vintage cars from the sixties. They just have a really NOSTALGIC, HAPPY feel about them. **How big is your collection?** About 50 to 60 cars! **It sounds like you dig a vintage vibe in general?** Older things have a lot more personality — I love that you can just tell that time has passed. I always think, 'WHO HAD IT BEFORE ME, WHERE HAS IT BEEN, & WHAT HAS IT HEARD & SEEN?' And most of them are older than you are - it's such a bizarre concept, isn't it? To have something in your hand that is older than you! **What has been your best vintage find?** I didn't buy it, but my mum had an old VW convertible Beetle for a few years. I had a Vespa at the time and I was always like, "I don't need a driver's license for a car!". But when she got the car, I was like, "ok, so maybe I do need it!" So I got my license and DROVE IT AROUND SWITZERLAND ALL SUMMER LONG **So you're from Switzerland - tell us about your hometown.** Oh - it's a little hole in the middle of nowhere! A valley, surrounded by two chains of mountains lost between France, Germany and Switzerland. It's ten minutes from each country, so it was never a big deal crossing a border for me. It's a beautiful region and I like going back to take pictures - and I do miss it. I just could never live there again. I've just always felt like I don't fit in and NEEDED TO GO SOMEWHERE ELSE. I think that's where my passion for always going somewhere else and exploring comes from. **So you love travelling?** I CAN'T SIT STILL! **How often do you go road tripping?** I think I'm gone like twice a month, sometimes once a week! I must have gone on over a hundred road trips. If there's been a week that I haven't been anywhere, then I kind of beg my boyfriend to take the car and just go somewhere on a Sunday. Even if it's just a shorter drive, I just want to be on the road and discover something new. It's really addictive. I mean, SO MANY PLACES, AND SO LITTLE TIME | **What is it that you love about being on the road?** You find out things about yourself that you wouldn't when you're constantly having to do things that you don't want to do. You have the freedom to do whatever you want to do, and be whoever you want to be. >

When you are on the road, you sort of have that anonymity, LIKE YOU'RE FREE & NOT BEING WATCHED. **Tell us about some of your best road trips.** Two years ago, I did a road trip with my dad to the Isle of Skye in Scotland. It was our first holiday back together and it was all about photography and being on the road. I also loved road tripping when I was living in Switzerland - I had just moved to a new area and I didn't know anyone there. So it was JUST ME, MY CAR & MY DOG, CHARLIE. We went driving everywhere and anywhere around in the countryside - I kind of miss that! **What's your absolute favourite location?** It's really hard to pick one place because I've travelled so much, but Puglia - it's the heel of the boot of Italy. It's just one of the most gorgeous places I've ever been to. **And the most awesome road you've driven?** It's definitely the road in Scotland that goes from Inverness all the way to the Isle of Skye. Actually all the roads on Isle of Skye - they're so cool because they're all one-way roads and sometimes you have to stop because sheep just appear and cross in front of you. **What could you not live without on the road?** MUSIC. OH- & MY CAMERA! **What's on your playlist?** There's one artist I could listen to non-stop: Ben Howard. I think even more so than The Beatles and The Beach Boys. **You have a thing for artists that start with B!** Hey - yeah! Haha, I've never realised that! **So you obviously love your music - and we heard that you title your pictures after musicians?** Yes, I title them from lyrics of my favourite songs. Since I'm obsessed with Ben Howard, Mumford & Sons and those sort of musicians, there are quite a few images named after them. MUSIC IS A BIG PART OF EVERYTHING I DO, especially when I'm on the road. If I don't have music in the car, it's just not the same experience. It's a big, big part of my creative process in general. It just gets you in your own little world, another way to escape. And I think that's what all my pictures are about - lots of little moments of escape really. **Who's your best travel buddy?** I would choose MY DOG. HE IS ACTUALLY A REALLY GREAT TRAVEL BUDDY. But he's got a really weird music taste, he doesn't like Ben Howard. He cries every time he hears a man's voice - I'm serious! He prefers women's voices, like Adele and Taylor Swift. I also have to say I LOVE TRAVELLING WITH MY FRIENDS. I love finding ourselves back together, cruising on the road and just catching up on each other's lives. We've known each other for so long that we're comfortable doing whatever we want - like singing on

JUST ME, MY CAR
& MY DOG, CHARLIE

the top of our voices and that sort of thing. It's special every time - those little moments you can remember forever. **What's the most dramatic situation you've been in with the small cars?** OH - I'VE HAD A FEW! One of the first was when I got my very first toy car. I left it outside my mum's office and someone reversed over it! It was completely crushed! At the time I was really close to crying as it was my first van, but now it's pretty hilarious. **Tell us about some of the funny situations you've been in.** Well, everyday really! When I'm taking pictures, people always ask, 'what the hell are you doing? Are you ok?', because I'm always laying on the ground to get a shot. **It sounds like you've clocked up quite a few miles! What advice do you have for fellow road trippers?** DON'T PLAN TOO MUCH! Have a rough idea of where you want to go, but don't be too specific because the best places are the ones you don't expect to see. JUST DRIVE & STOP WHEREVER YOU FEEL And try have the window open - to smell the place. Sometimes I even turn the music down if I'm in the woods so I can hear the birds or water. All those little things make a place what it is. **Any hidden locations you can share with us?** If you ever go to Scotland, you must go to a place called *The Fairy Glen*. Oh it's amazing! I just want to go back there - it's just one of these places you can explore non-stop and see so many hidden locations. It's out of this world. **What does wanderlust mean to you?** Ah... wanderlust - I love that word! I think it's a reason to get up every morning, always having that thirst for exploring, never taking things for granted and always wanting to see more. It doesn't mean you are never satisfied with what you have, you are just thirsty to see more. **We are in love with your photos! They're so dreamy and unique - like nothing else! Could you choose your favourite road trip photo to share with us?** (Blushing) Thank you! It's just like my little thing I'M NOT TRYING TO SAVE THE WORLD OR ANYTHING... but I think if you can make people smile and laugh and just make them happy - it's already a big step! ♥

FAVE BANDS: BEATLES & BEACH BOYS!

N⁰ 8

THE PEOPLE.

THE JOURNEY,

EIGHT

FROM

TO

START DATE

END DATE

BEFORE

THE IDEA FOR THIS ROAD TRIP POPPED UP WHEN

I'VE BEEN WANTING TO DO IT SINCE

IT'S GOING TO BE

I'M ROAD TRIPPING WITH

BECAUSE

I CAN'T WAIT TO

WE NEED TO ORGANISE

N.º 8

THE PLANNED ROUTE IS

FUN THINGS WE'RE PLANNING

ADVICE AND TIPS I GATHERED BEFORE THE TRIP

Date:
Place:

THE FIRST DAY OF THIS TRIP HAS BEEN

WE STARTED IN

ALONG THE WAY, WE STOPPED

WE ENDED AT

MY FEELINGS AS WE DEPARTED

IN THE CAR WE

PLACES WE ATE AT

THE EVENING WAS SPENT

MY BED TONIGHT

Nº 8

snap happy

the Wheels

LOOK

SMELL

SOUNDS

BORN IN

MODEL

OWNED BY

FUEL EFFICIENCY

COOL FACTOR

BEST PART

I WISH THAT

WE HEREBY NAME THIS CAR

ON THE ROAD

Take a detour
down a road
that looks
interesting.

{"image_type":"ornament","description":"decorative arrow pointing right"}

Date:

Place:

WE'VE NOW BEEN ON THE ROAD FOR   DAYS

TODAY I WOKE UP IN   AT   AM/PM

MY SLEEP WAS

I DREAMED ABOUT

I BRUSHED MY TEETH IN

THE SHOWER WAS

I DRESSED IN

THE MORNING WAS SPENT

IN THE AFTERNOON, WE

THE EVENING WAS

the cutest...

PERSON

TOWN

SIGN

most random...

STOP

TOPIC

MEAL

Coolest...

PERSONALITY

STOP

DISCOVERY

today...

I WOKE UP

I WENT

I FELT

I ATE

I DRANK

I SAW

I SAT

I WORKED

I HEARD

I FOUND

I DESIRED

I RAN

I DECIDED

I UNDERSTOOD

I DROOLED OVER

I SLEPT

IMAGE: @VIVIANNEFLRS

Date:

Place:

TODY IS DAY   OF THE TRIP AND THE ODOMETER READS

WE ARE CURRENTLY

THE CAR IS LOOKING LIKE

I CAN'T FIND MY

CAR RULES WE'VE MADE

THINGS WE LAUGH ABOUT

THINGS WE TALK ABOUT

THINGS WE DEBATE

THREE PEOPLE (DEAD OR ALIVE) THAT I'VE LOVE TO GO ROAD TRIPPING WITH AND WHY

WORDS WE OVERUSE

MUSIC ON REPEAT

BEST BREAKFAST

MOST WICKED DINNER SPOT

COMFIEST BED

EXERCISE WE'VE DONE

HIDDEN GEMS WE'VE FOUND

NATURE WE'VE EXPLORED

IF MY BODY COULD TALK, IT WOULD SAY

MY TRAVEL BUDDIES

NAME

RIGHT NOW, HE/SHE LOOKS LIKE

BEST PERSONALITY TRAITS

FAVOURITE SONG

SOMETHING ANNOYING ABOUT HIM/HER

IN THE CAR, HE/SHE

FAVOURITE MOMENT TOGETHER

NAME

WE'VE KNOWN EACH OTHER SINCE

I LOVE THAT HE/SHE

I CAN'T BELIEVE THAT HE/SHE

HE/SHE ALWAYS EATS

I WILL ALWAYS REMEMBER

HIS/HER FAVOURITE MOMENT ON THE TRIP WAS

NAME

I WOULD DESCRIBE HIM/HER AS

THE BEST THING ABOUT HIM/HER

HE/SHE UPSETS ME WHEN

A SPECIAL MOMENT WE HAD

WE LAUGHED AT

SOMETHING I DON'T KNOW ABOUT HIM/HER *(go & ask!)*

Nº 8

MY LAST 24 HOURS

TEN THINGS THAT MAKE ME SMILE

On this trip...

I SAID YES TO

I SAID NO TO

I FOUND IT INTERESTING THAT

I AM GLAD THAT I SPOKE TO

I ENJOYED EATING

I GOT IN TROUBLE WHEN

I WAS STOKED TO EXPERIENCE

WHAT I LEARNED ABOUT MYSELF

WHAT I LEARNED ABOUT SOMEONE ELSE

AMAZING PEOPLE WHO HELPED US ALONG THE WAY

BEST SING-ALONG MOMENT

AN AWESOME MEMORY

AND THE WORST *(but is now a funny story to tell)*

I'M GRATEFUL I PACKED

THE THINGS I NEVER USED

I WAS WARM WHEN

I WAS FREEZING WHEN

i want to live by the ocean ...

but also in the forest.
but also in the mountains.
but also in a big city.
but also in the countryside.

... you feel me?

Moments...

Pick some
wild flowers
and give them
to a stranger.

Nº 8

the Travel Bug

Its a tale of a 54 year romance, a VW beetle,
188,000 miles, and an epic road trip across continents.
Meet Beth and Ivan Hodge, a love struck couple
who challenged convention and set off on a once-in-a-lifetime
adventure from London to New Zealand, via Calcutta - twice

It was the very start of the swinging sixties, Europe's Golden Age, the year that The Beatles formed and a time when a loaf of bread cost five pence. It was also a time when couples got married and settled down with kids and white picket fences, a world where air travel was out of reach for many, and overseas travel was simply unconventional. But for the newly-wed New Zealanders in their twenties, the world was their oyster and the road less travelled was beckoning to be explored.

After a honeymoon that took them to Sydney and then all the way to London, the pair were bitten hard by the travel bug. Instead of returning home and buying a house like tradition called for, the young couple purchased a VW Beetle for £430, and set off for what was to be an adventure of epic proportions. The road trip lasted for more than three months, spanning across Europe, the Middle East and India, coming to an end in New Zealand after a seven-week cargo boat trip from Calcutta.

Living in a world before GPS, Lonely Planet guides and the internet, the couple ventured across untouched landscapes and into the unknown. They knew little about cultures, laws and religions – there were no guide books or resources to refer to – so they simply learned everything along the way.

"We had maps for Europe, but no maps for Turkey," Beth reminisces. "Going into the desert was exciting. We didn't know anything about it. We only had strip maps that told us where the petrol barrels were".

As adventure unfolded, Beth and Ivan gathered a wealth of rare experiences. Some of their best memories include attending the Queen's Garden Party in London, camping outside the Taj Mahal to watch the sunrise, entertaining tribal children in Iran with their tape recorder and exploring rough terrain that would eventually be rocked by political instability. They even ran out of petrol in the middle of nowhere - in dangerous places that they'd been warned about being attacked by nomads.

For some, the couple's incredible journey would have been enough adventure to last a lifetime. But for Beth and Ivan, it was just the beginning, and 35 years later in 1996 they decided to dust off the Beetle and retrace their tracks.

With stars in their eyes, hearts filled with love and a desire to be free on the road again, they embarked on the same road trip – for the second time.

Looking at the world with a new perspective but the same youthful sense of adventure, the pair got to see changes in cultures, the impact of new technology, the decay of communism, the transformation of political landscapes and the evolution of society in countries like Iran and Turkey. And through it all, weathering rough terrain and harsh desert conditions, The Beetle carried Beth and Ivan home safely – on both occasions.

Now in their eighties with awe-inspiring stories of trailblazing, a treasure trove of memories and a published book, *For Love and a Beetle*, the couple are living proof that it's never too late to chase adventure and live out your dreams.

SO IVAN, AT 1.9 METRES, WE CAN'T REALLY DESCRIBE YOU AS A SMALL MAN. WHY DID YOU CHOOSE A BEETLE, OF ALL CARS, AS YOUR HOME? We didn't know much about cars, but Volkswagen seemed reliable and would make the long journey. We couldn't afford a Kombi - it was twice the price of a Beetle. It was good value for us and very comfortable.

WHAT WAS GOING THROUGH YOUR MINDS WHEN YOU FIRST SET OFF? *Beth* - We were just excited to go on an adventure. We had enough food, and we thought we knew enough, but we didn't really. We had a medical kit and a water purifier, so we knew we'd be alright. Then, we just set off.

WHAT WAS YOUR DAILY BUDGET ON YOUR FIRST TRIP? *Ivan* - We lived on £1 a day for our expenses and £1 a day for the car (petrol). >

IMAGES: IVAN AND BETH HODGE

THAT DOESN'T SOUND LIKE MUCH! WHERE DID YOU SPEND THE NIGHTS? *Beth* - We would sleep in our car or camp underneath the stars. We stopped in small villages - the police sometimes saw us and offered to let us sleep in their compound for safety. We were always just trying to find a place that we felt secure.

TWO PEOPLE SLEEPING IN A BEETLE, IT DOESN'T SOUND TOO COMFORTABLE? *Ivan* - Actually, the seats in the Beetle were very comfortable. They were wide and when you put down the back, it lay flat. We packed tins of fruit underneath it so that it was firm. We would then cover it with two sleeping bags, and Beth made curtains to go around the windows. So it was really very comfortable.
Beth - We weren't used to all the comforts you have now with beds, spring mattresses and all the rest of it. That's all we had - we couldn't ask for anything else.

YOU TRAVELLED THROUGH SOME PRETTY UNTOUCHED AREAS. WHAT DID YOU EAT ALONG THE WAY? *Beth* - We had a gas cooker with us and would cook as much as we could. We would only get fruit that you could peel.
Ivan - We ate lots of spaghetti because it was cheap, spam and baked beans, and lots of bread. Travelling on the road also taught us to have our tea without milk and we wouldn't drink the water unless we purified it.

WHERE DID YOU STOP TO EAT ALONG THE WAY? *Ivan* - Meals were always an occasion to us. We'd always make them special wherever we were, so we'd pull out the table, place the tablecloth down and add fresh flowers on top. Beth loved to pick flowers along the way.

WHAT WAS THE BEST THING ABOUT BEING ON THE ROAD? *Beth* - Absolute freedom. Freedom to do what you like is brilliant. No constraints, no deadlines, nobody telling you what to do.

the hodges

WHAT WAS YOUR FAVOURITE POSSESSION YOU TOOK WITH YOU? *Beth -* My green handbag! It was avocado green. It was a very 'in' colour at the time - one of those hard ones with a handle. It always hung on the hand grip inside the car and it swung so much that it rubbed the paint off.

WHAT MUSIC DID YOU LISTEN TO IN THE CAR? *Ivan -* We didn't have a radio but we had a tape recorder that we used to document our journey, so we would make tape recordings of music we enjoyed, usually from the shows we had seen on the West End.

A MOMENT WHEN YOU HAD TO PINCH YOURSELF *Ivan -* In Northern India, when we drove to Kashmir. Dharamshala is beautiful. The altitude, the mountains, and the people are all there to worship, so the whole atmosphere around you is very spiritual and calm. It was very special.

THE WILDEST PLACE YOU SLEPT? *Ivan -* In the middle of the desert, one morning we woke up surrounded by a dozen nomads just staring at us. *Beth -* We must have looked so curious.

ANY HAIRY MOMENTS? *Beth -* I still laugh at this time in Turkey when Ivan drove around the corner and ran into a donkey. We weren't used to seeing anything on the road and we came around a winding, dirt road where there was a peasant man and his donkey - we hit the brakes and the car slid. The donkey was okay - he only got a bump in the rump! *Ivan -* Well, we ran out of petrol a few times. The quality of petrol was very bad in some countries and it often didn't get us as far as we thought it would. That was a serious situation because we were in the middle of nowhere, and there was very little traffic going past.

THE MOST BEAUTIFUL PLACE YOU WOKE UP IN? *Ivan -* The Taj Mahal - it's a love story. We went and sat on that seat, where Lady Di sat on her own. After we visited there, we drove around the back overlooking the water. We wanted to see the moonlight on the Taj Mahal, but there was no moon visible that night. So instead, we camped and woke up early to see the sunrise.

YOUR PHOTOS ARE AMAZING, WHAT CAMERA DID YOU USE? *Ivan -* We weren't photographers, but we had a second hand Voigtländer camera that had a very good lens. We couldn't afford the film though, so we were very careful with the amount of photos we took.

WHAT DID LIFE ON THE ROAD TEACH YOU? *Ivan -* Every day you're driving, the moment you start, it's a new experience. You're always looking forward, you're not looking back.

YOUR THREE TIPS FOR LIFE ON THE ROAD. *1.* Travel early in the day. It's so clear, lovely and crisp. *2.* Don't travel too far in a day. *3.* Don't expect to travel to fast. Don't be in a hurry.

AFTER SO MANY ADVENTURES, YOU DECIDED TO DONATE THE BEETLE TO THE MOTAT MUSEUM IN NEW ZEALAND, WAS IT HARD TO LET GO OF? *Beth -* No, it's not fast enough for the modern roads. We realise it's in the best place, it will be loved and we can go visit it. *Ivan -* We don't miss it because of all it has given us, we have maximised our pleasure of the car. ♥

See more of Ivan and Beth Hodge
www.forloveandabeetle.com

people I met

roads I loved

cities & towns discovered

funny moments

BIG SUR, CALIFORNIA, USA

the road less *travelled*

Pack up the car, roll down the windows, crank up the tunes and get wonderfully lost along some of the world's most spellbinding roads and routes.

TROLLSTIGEN, AKA 'TROLL LADDER' *Norway*
Take a trip down the 'Troll Ladder', a winding road nestled in the Norwegian mountains. Known by locals as the 'Trolls Path', it includes eleven hairpin bends and steep inclines, boasting epic views of Scandinavia's best scenery.

GREAT OCEAN ROAD *Victoria, Australia*
One of the most beautiful roads in Australia takes you on a journey that wraps around sea cliffs to some of the most iconic surf spots, rainforest walks, fishing villages and the spectacular natural Twelve Apostles limestone rock formations.

TIANMEN MOUNTAIN ROAD *Hunan, China*
Famous for its '99 bends' on the road up to Tianmen Cave, this drive is full of sharp turns along vertical cliffs. It's definitely not for the faint-hearted, but worth it for the jaw-dropping mountain views.

HIGHWAY 1, AKA 'BIG SUR' *California, USA*
Feel those laid-back Californian vibes along this iconic 85 mile drive between San Francisco and Los Angeles. Beautiful seaside villages, remote beaches and staggering views over perilous cliffs will make you want to stop at least a dozen times along the way.

WEST COAST DRIVE *South Island, New Zealand*
With contrasting landscapes of untouched seaside vistas, glaciers, lush vegetation and the unearthly Punakaiki Pancake Rocks, this scenic drive along the rugged West Coast is one of the best ways to see the South Island.

THE RING ROAD, (HIGHWAY 1) *Iceland*
A lap of Iceland on the Ring Road offers one of the most volatile landscapes on earth. Frozen glaciers, volcanoes, waterfalls, geo-thermal pools, spouting geysers, canyons, snow-capped mountains and iceberg-filled glacial lagoons are just some of the diverse views you'll encounter.

TIANMEN MOUNTAIN ROAD, CHINA

AMALFI COAST ROUTE *Italy*
Dazzling drivers with its mysterious grottos and shimmering bays, this popular route hugs the shoreline from Sorrento to Salerno against a backdrop of pastel-coloured architecture.

ROUTE DES GRANDES ALPES *France*
This spectacular road will make you feel like you're on set of a James Bond movie. You'll twist and wind your way north from the French Riviera to Lake Geneva through the French Alps, one dramatic mountain pass after another (17 if you care to count)!

RUTA 40 *Argentina*
This legendary road is one of the longest stretches of highway in the world, crossing eighteen rivers and connecting twenty national parks. You'll pass through pristine lakes, bustling cities and diverse landscapes.

SEVEN MILE BRIDGE *Florida Keys, USA*
You'll feel like you're in a seaplane about to take off into the air when cruising along this floating road of bridges, with coral, limestone islands, and some of the most exquisite waters in the world right underneath your wheels!

ICEFIELDS PARKWAY *Canada*
This picturesque stretch of road passes through two national parks between Lake Louise and Jasper via Banff, wowing drivers with spectacular glaciers, waterfalls, lakes and endless rocky peaks along the way.

ROUTE 66 *USA*
The most famous and beloved road in the USA runs through eight states from the East to the West Coast. Once the main route from Chicago to California, and for some a pathway to the American dream, it is now a classic journey through small town America.

CHAPMAN'S PEAK DRIVE *Cape Town, South Africa*
Hailed as one of the most scenic areas of South Africa, this drive combines panoramic views of Cape Town and its pristine coastline. If you're lucky, it's also the perfect route for spotting dolphins, whales and monkeys!

STELVIO PASS *Italy*
This legendary slice of road straddles the Swiss-Italian border with its notorious wall of 48 treacherous bends between Bormio and Stilfs.

THE ATLANTIC ROAD *Norway*
It's like you're island hopping, but on the road! With some of the world's most unusual bridges, this quirky road in the midwest part of the Norwegian coastline will take you on a unique journey.

N222, PESO DA RÉGUA TO PINHÃO *Portugal*
This little known route is a local secret and a favourite amongst wine lovers. With 27 kilometres of stunning views over terraced hills, the road conveniently ends at the small port wine town, Pinhao, where you can taste the wonderful flavours of this beautiful region.

MONUMENT VALLEY SCENIC DRIVE
Navajo Tribal Park, Arizona, USA
This sacred red sand desert region on the Arizona-Utah border is known for the towering sandstone buttes of Monument Valley Navajo Tribal Park. Get your skateboard ready to ride down the flat road - it doesn't get more idyllic than this!

THE DEATH ROAD *Bolivia*
With a 5000ft descent, steep drops and an average of 300 deaths per year, this terrifying route is popular with cyclists and has been voted as one of the most dangerous roads in the world.

HĀNA HIGHWAY *Maui Island, Hawaii, USA*
Discover the 'real' Hawaii along this earthy route. You'll pass by lush, raw landscapes, stunning waterfalls, exotic local fruit stands, and stop for a dip at one of the picture-perfect black sand beaches.

GUOLIANG TUNNEL ROAD *China*
Entirely built by local villagers through a rocky cliff in the Taihang Mountains, this spectacular but dangerous tunnel is carved along the edge of a mountain that links the Guoliang village to the outside world. ♥

Secret Swimming Spots

HAVASU FALLS, SUPA
ARIZONA, USA

From mysterious underwater caves to shimmering hidden pools, these untouched, natural water holes around the world are enough to entice you to run away with your swimsuit!

PAMUKKALE THERMAL POOLS *Turkey*
With a name that literally translates to 'cotton castle' in Turkish, these thermal pools are filled with natural hot spring waters that cascade down travertine terraces onto a nearby hillside. For thousands of years, people have come to bathe in these mineral-rich thermal waters.

CENOTE IK-KIL (NEAR CHICHÉN ITZÁ) *Mexico*
Named by the ancient Mayans, this is one of the most incredible swimming holes in the world. Located 85 miles below the ground and surrounded by hanging vines, you'll be submerged into these mystical waters created by collapsed limestone.

CLUE D'AIGLUN *Alpes-Maritimes, France*
Located in the mountains just outside the buzz of the French Riviera, is an aquatic playground brimming with vivid turquoise pools, waterfalls, clear rivers, water chutes, bubbling natural jacuzzis, secret grottos and rock passages.

THE WATERFALLS OF KRKA NATIONAL PARK *Croatia*
Sitting on the jagged coastline of Croatia is this extraordinary National Park, home to stunning trails and the spectacular Krka waterfalls. Get lost along the lush paths, soak up the sunshine, and spend the day swimming in this relatively untouched natural haven.

GOD'S BATH *Sonora, California, USA*
You'll find this stunning swimming hole at the end of a long, winding road in the Californian foothills. After some rock-hopping and wading upstream, you'll jump off the granite bridge, swim beneath it and pop out in a hole milled out by the stream.

TEA TREES LAKE *Byron Bay, Australia*
One of Byron Bay's best kept secrets, Tea Tree Lake is an idyllic spot where locals go to rejuvenate their body, mind and soul. Supernatural oils from the Tea Tree plants drop into the water, creating a medical bath that works magic on your skin.

JOSEPHINE FALLS NATURAL WATER-SLIDE *Cairns, Australia*
Swim in crystal clear waters, relax on sandy banks and embrace your inner child on a natural waterslide in this stunning rainforest sanctuary.

**FIGURE 8 POOLS
AUSTRALIA**

HAVASU FALLS, SUPAI *Arizona, USA*
Be captivated for hours by this magical spot, located at the base of the Grand Canyon. Leap off the waterfall, swim, horse ride, camp or hike - whatever takes your fancy, you won't want to leave!

WALCHENSEE *Bavaria, Germany*
Walchensee is one of the deepest, purest and largest alpine lakes in Bavaria. With sapphire blue, drinking-quality water, it's the perfect spot to cool down on a hot summers day.

MADISON BLUE SPRINGS *Florida, USA*
Energise your body and soul as you slip into this hidden limestone basin, filled with refreshing, clear spring water along the banks of the Withlacoochee River.

PARADISE VALLEY *Morocco*
A hippy hangout in the 60's and one of Jimi Hendrix's favourite retreats, this deep, palm-lined canyon in the Moroccan High Atlas Mountains has it all. Carved out over thousands of years by waterfalls, you'll stumble upon flowing streams, plunge pools, limestone gorges, rich plantations and charming villages.

BRONTE ROCK POOL *Sydney, Australia*
On the edge of this beachside suburb in Sydney is a magical escape from the hustle and bustle of city life. Let all your worries wash away while swimming laps as the sun rises over the seaside pool, or take an evening dip while the ocean crashes against the shore.

SHIRAHONE-ONSEN HOT SPRING *Japan*
In a deep gorge 1,400 meters above sea level, lies this milky-white water hot spring that will make you feel like you're floating on a cloud.

FLUME WATER SLIDE
Waimea, Trailhead, Hawaii, USA
Hidden in this jungle paradise is the world's coolest waterslide! You'll have to hike through steamy forests, a darkened tunnel and some cliff-side paths to get here, but it's well worth the reward.

KUANG SI FALLS *Luang Prabang, Laos*
Swing like Tarzan from vines and splash into this spectacular natural azure pool. With trails surrounding this tropical jungle, you can climb to the top where you'll see the stream feeding into the falls.

BIMMAH SINKHOLE *Oman*
Follow concrete stairs into this amazing limestone hollow, created by natural erosion and the collapse of surrounding rocks.

FIGURE 8 POOLS,
Royal National Park, NSW, Australia
These naturally formed rock pools are tucked between coastal headlands in Sydney's Royal National Park. It's quite a hike to find them and only safe to visit during low tide - but it's worth the adventure!

TO SUA OCEAN TRENCH *Upolu Island, Samoa*
An idyllic spot located in Samoa's Lotofaga village, the To Sua Ocean trench is surrounded by beautiful, manicured gardens with views spanning across the Pacific Ocean. Climb down the ladder and dive into the magnificent turquoise waters.

REYKJADALUR *Iceland Hot Springs*
Directly translating to 'steam valley', Reykjadalur holds true to its name with clouds of white mist floating in every direction. After hiking in this remote part of the world, a dip in a natural hot spring is the perfect way to unwind.

GROTTO OF POETRY *Rocca Vecchia, Italy*
Cliff jump off this slice of paradise into crystal-clear waters, while surrounded by breathtaking scenery. This spot may not be easy to reach, but it's definitely worth the effort. ♥

Bucket list festivals

Whether you're into music, the arts, yoga, beer, experiencing different cultures or something a little more quirky, festivals add another layer to your road tripping experience. Feel the energy and let your destination come alive at these must-visit festivals around the globe.

SECRET SOLSTICE *Reykjavik, Iceland*
With a country that has produced artists like Sigur Rós and Björk, it's no surprise that Iceland also plays host to some of the world's best music festivals. Secret Solstice is one of them, bringing big name artists together inside a glacier across three days of uninterrupted sunlight.

BURNING MAN *Black Rock City, Nevada, USA*
Each year, tens of thousands of artists and art enthusiasts make the pilgrimage to Black Rock City (a temporary metropolis in the Nevada desert) for this iconic celebration of art, culture and self-expression.

GLASTONBURY FESTIVAL *Somerset, UK*
Glastonbury is one of the world's most iconic music festivals and should be on everyone's bucketlists. Boasting incredible music lineups during the English summer, the five day festival also offers the best of comedy, dance theatre and circus. Pack your gumboots - it's famous for being muddy!

COACHELLA VALLEY MUSIC FESTIVAL *Indio, California USA*
This world-famous, epic music and arts festival is a staple event in every music lover's calendar. Set in the Californian desert over two weekends, the biggest names in music draw half a million people from around the globe every year.

HOLI FESTIVAL *India*
Experience India at its happiest in this hilarious festival of colours that celebrates the beginning of spring. The festival is a crazy spectacle to witness - be sure to wear clothes that you don't mind ruining as the crowds throw coloured powders your way!

OKTOBERFEST *Bavaria, Germany*
Strap on your lederhosen and get ready for the world's largest Volkfest (beer festival and travelling funfair). This sixteen day festival attracts more than six million people from around the world!

WORLD BODY PAINTING FESTIVAL *Portschach, Austria*
A colourful spectacle not to be missed! The art of body painting comes alive during this vibrant event that draws some of the world's most talented artists together to celebrate art, music and fashion.

WORLD BUSKERS FESTIVAL *Christchurch, NZ*
From circus acts, comedians, musicians, burlesque and acrobats, the best of the world's sidewalks come together in this celebration of quirky and eccentric street performers.

ENVISION FESTIVAL *Costa Rica*
Music, nature, mindfulness and happy souls come together in this epic four day festival offering live performances, seminars, yoga, workshops, and locally sourced food.

SUNDANCE FILM FESTIVAL *Utah, USA*
America's most famous film festival is a special combination of show and snow. Pack your blanket, a picnic and sit under the stars during this annual celebration of independent film making.

STONEHENGE SUMMER SOLSTICE *Wiltshire, UK*
This four day camping, music and beer festival attracts druids, hippies, New Age prophets and mystery seekers together to worship the sun during the northern hemisphere's shortest night of the year.

BUKTA FESTIVAL
Telegrafbukta Beach, Tromso, Norway
This open-air music festival is a celebration of rock music, seafood and beer. Set on a beach, surrounded by a woodland park with snow-capped mountains and the glittering Arctic Ocean as a backdrop, The Bukta Festival wins the prize for most surreal location!

LIGHTING IN A BOTTLE *Bradley, California, USA*
A magical festival that brings together visionary and healing arts, self-awareness and some of the world's biggest and most progressive names in music. This six day art, music and yoga festival has also been hailed as the most 'green' and environmentally conscious in America.

TOMORROWLAND *Boom, Belgium*
Hailed as an electronic mecca for lovers of EDM, Tomorrowland takes place between Antwerp and Brussels and is one of the biggest electronic festivals in the world.

NEW ORLEANS JAZZ FESTIVAL *Louisiana, USA*
Spanning across ten days, this world famous festival has celebrated the rich cultural heritage of the original birth place of jazz for over four decades.

SHAKTI FEST *Joshua Tree, California, USA*
This five day yoga festival in a picturesque setting celebrates the divine feminine through personal growth workshops, yoga, meditation and sacred music.

SPLENDOUR IN THE GRASS
Byron Bay, NSW, Australia
Located in the beautiful coastal town of Byron Bay, Splendour in the Grass is one of Australia's most famous music festivals, and plays host to some of the biggest international and local names in music.

PORT ELIOT FESTIVAL *Cornwall, UK*
Set on the grassy pastures around Port Eliot House, an eclectic mix of musicians, poets, writers and filmmakers come together in this colourful celebration of creative arts.

AFRIKABURN
Tankwa Karoo National Park, South Africa
Africa's unique version of the infamous Burning Man festival sees thousands of festival goers dressed in elaborate costumes and body paint gather in the arid Karoo semi-desert. Over six days, creativity, art, music and self-expression is celebrated in this unusual event.

LEVITATION *Carson Creek Ranch, Austin, Texas, USA*
Let go of reality and immerse yourself in three days of psychedelic rock alongside the Colorado River. Formally known as the Austin Psych Fest, the festival was inspired by the creative art and music explosion of the 1960s and attracts the likes of The Flaming Lips and Tame Impala. ♥

Explore
the road by foot...

QUIRAING ISLE OF SKYE, SCOTLAND

Some of the most beautiful places on earth are often only accessible by foot. Park the car and get your walking shoes ready for one of these epic hikes!

FIMMVÖRÐU HÁLS PASS *Iceland*
This 25 kilometre hike is beautiful, breathtaking and tough. You'll pass through colourful volcanic terrain, green valleys, black sands, snowfields, icy lakes and hot springs, reaching the famous Skógafoss waterfall and glittering white Eyjafjallajökull glacier.

GRINDELWALD *Switzerland*
You'll feel like you stepped right into a scene of *The Sound of Music* in this truly breathtaking green hollow. Surrounded by snowy white mountain peaks, there are 300 kilometres of walking trails between three world famous mountains.

SERNYIRTO AZZURRO *Cinque Terre, Italy*
Be charmed by the colourful buildings, vineyards, cliff jumps and swimming spots along this beautiful walk that takes you through five old seaside fishing villages along the Italian Riviera.

QUIRAING ISLE OF SKYE *Scotland*
Wander for up to five hours through this magnificent terrain, formed by a huge landslip. You'll pass high cliffs, green hills and hidden plateaus along this 6.8 kilometre loop.

DOSEWALLIPS RIVER TRAIL
Olympic National Park, Washington
Get lost along this beautiful trail full of wild flowers and pine trees as you hike along the the Dosewallips River.

KALALAU TRAIL *Kauai, Hawaii, USA*
Spread over eleven miles in a lush rain forest, this cliff trail will be one of the most exhilarating treks you'll ever experience as you pass by waterfalls, beaches, rivers and snack on fresh guavas!

ZION NARROWS *Utah, USA*
Take your swimsuit with you on this canyon hike as you make your way along the Virgin River. The hike can be done in a day, but camping overnight under the stars will give you the full experience.

SEQUOIA NATIONAL PARK *California, USA*
Feel how small you really are when you hug the world's biggest trees! These grand giants are thousands of years old and are set amongst a range of amazing hikes around the park, taking you through waterfalls, the historic Moro Rock, canyons and breathtaking lookouts.

TOUR DU MONT BLANC
France, Italy, and Switzerland
Take on Europe's infamous long distance trek across the borders of three countries, and be swept away by the alpine charm of lakes, valleys and glaciers.

HOLLYWOOD SIGN *LA, California, USA*
Why take a picture from afar when you can get up close and personal to one of the most famous signs in the world? Choose one of three routes and see Los Angeles from a different perspective.

LAGUNA DE LOS TRES *Argentina*
You'll pass through the most picturesque, rugged mountain terrain in Patagonia for seven to nine hours, before reaching the majestic Fitz Roy summit and it's shimmering, turquoise lake.

TIJUCA FOREST HIKE *Rio de Janeiro, Brazil*
There's no better way to view the entire city of Rio de Janeiro than taking on this hike through the largest urban forest in the world, straight to the top of Tijuca Peak.

BAY OF FIRES *Tasmania, Australia*
Regarded as one of Australia's most beautiful locations, you'll be mesmerised by 50 kilometres of dreamy white sands, crystal blue waters and orange-hued boulder rocks.

QUEEN CHARLOTTE TRACK *New Zealand*
A 70 km stretch in the magical Marlborough Sounds, you'll need three to five days to experience this phenomenal hike amongst waterfalls, lush terrain and lofty peaks . If you're feeling extra adventurous, head off in a kayak across the sparkling blue waters.

TROLLTUNGA *Norway*
With one of the most spectacular views in the world, the steep hike to Trolltunga is one you can't pass up. You'll trek through a stunning mountain landscape before reaching this scenic overhanging cliff top.

CONWAY CIRCUIT *Whitsunday Islands, Australia*
In the heart of the Great Barrier Reef lies the Whitsunday Islands. Explore it's iconic aqua waters and lush, tropical landscape while you wind through walking trails in the Conway National Park.

BONDI TO COOGEE *Sydney, Australia*
Located on the edge of Sydney's Eastern suburbs, this is a coastal walk like no other! The trail starts at Australia's most famous beach, Bondi, and takes on mesmerising cliff-side twists and turns alongside jagged bays, sandy beaches and hidden rock pools, all the way to Coogee beach.

SHIPWRECK TRAIL
Cape Point Nature Reserve, South Africa
Take on the rocky and dramatic coastline near the southern most point in Africa, where the deserted shoreline is littered with historical shipwrecks. Surrounded by thick vegetation, you may even be accompanied by Bontebok, mountain zebras and baboons!

HUA SHAN (MOUNT HUA) *China*
Considered the most dangerous hiking trail in the world and home to several influential Taoist temples, this historical trek features a network of trails, narrow stairs, steep drops, and vertical passes. Built by monks, nuns and pilgrims to reach the mountain's peaks, this area has been considered holy since the second century.

DANA TO PETRA *Jordan*
Voted by National Geographic as one of the world's best treks, this incredible five to nine day route takes you through four biosphere climates and the untouched wonders of Jordan. ♥

Off the beaten track

The weird, the whacky and the downright quirky: Spots around the world that have to be seen to be believed.

THE HJORUNDEFJORD SWING *Trandal, Norway*
Take a ride on the wildest swing in the world! Situated next to a fairytale-like treehouse in a remote, roadless village, you'll need to head over the mountains or arrive by sea to get there.

GLOUCESTER TREE *Pemberton, W.A. Australia*
For all the thrill seeking tree climbers out there: in the middle of the West Australian wilderness you'll find a tree full of pegs that spiral 61 metres to the top.

COSTA NOVA, AVEIRO *Portugal*
This quaint little fishing village is lined with an array of rainbow striped beach shacks. If there's somewhere in the world you'll make friends with the Mad Hatter, fly on a magic carpet, or brush your hair with a fork, it must be here!

PRADA HOUSE *Marfa, Texas, USA.*
What's the last thing you'd expect to find smack-bang in the middle of the desert? If your guess was a Prada store, then you're right. This luxury boutique, which is really more of an art installation, is sure to surprise many drivers passing through the Lone Star State.

PINK LAKE *Western Australia, Australia*
Is it a milkshake, or a lake? You won't believe your eyes seeing this pretty pink body of water in the middle of an island in the Recherche Archipelago.

SALVATION MOUNTAIN *California, USA*
Take half a million gallons of paint, a mountain and a happy artist living in his truck - and you get an epic, candy-coloured mountain in the middle of the Californian desert.

OATMAN *Arizona, USA*
This quirky town has a gold-mine tour, Wild West shootouts and an annual egg-frying contest - but it's the unusual habitation of donkeys that everyone comes to see. Chilling out in cafes, wandering into shops and peeking through windows, these wild creatures even have right of way on the roads.

TUNNEL OF LOVE *Klevan, Ukraine*
Get lost along this romantic old railway tunnel, found deep within a lush green forest. The three kilometre passageway is made up of natural green arches, and is a popular spot for lovers to make a wish.

LABYRINTH OF VILLA PISANI
Il Labirinto Stra, Italy
Love a challenge? Why not get completely lost in Venice? Created in 1720, this complex nine layer maze in Stra is hailed as the most difficult in the world to solve - even Napoleon was floored by the challenge.

CAPPADOCIA *Turkey*
Located in the historical region of Central Anatolia, is a dreamy landscape dotted with 'fairy chimneys' (rock formations) and hundreds of hot air balloons floating into the distance.

ZHANGYE DANXIA LANDFORM *China*

A result of red sandstone and mineral deposits being laid down over 24 million years, the 'Rainbow Mountains' are a kaleidoscope of colourful rock formations completely surreal to the eye.

CANCUN UNDERWATER MUSEUM
Cancun, Mexico

Why walk through a museum when you can swim? This crazy underwater world is home to over 500 sculptures across three submerged galleries.

NIMIS *Mölle, Sweden*

A labyrinth of rooms, corridors and towers, built solely by driftwood and rocks, this amazing micro-nation known as Ladonia is home to 17,000 citizens from more than 100 different countries!

COOBER PEDY SA, *Australia*

Have you ever dreamed of sleeping underground? In this old opal mining area an entire town has been built.under the earth to help residents escape harsh summer temperatures.

KUNSTHOFPASSAGE FUNNEL WALL
Dresden, Germany

If only the walls could talk… or sing? They do at the Kunsthofpassage Funnel wall! When the rain falls, this artistic drain system turns into music for your ears.

HUACACHINA *Peru*

Get your sand buggy ready! In the midst of one of the driest deserts in the world, you'll find this tiny oasis surrounded by palm trees, a tranquil lagoon and 96 residents. Legend has it that a mermaid inhabits the waters!

GOAT TREE, TAMRI *Morocco*

Do goats grow on trees? Well, in the small Village of Tamri, they seem to. Morocco's Argania trees are infested with nut-hungry goats, who climb like acrobats all over the trees in search of their favourite berries.

WISTERIA TUNNELS *Kawachi Fuji Gardens, Japan*

Get lost in the scents and beauty of the enchanting wisteria flower tunnels. Exploding with colour in all spectrums of purple, the two tunnels look more like a dream world than real life.

NEUSCHWANSTEIN CASTLE
Hohenschwangau, Germany

If you've ever felt like being a prince or princess for the day, a visit to this idyllic castle full of towers and spires will make you feel like you're in a real-life magical kingdom.

WAITOMO GLOW WORM CAVES
Otorohanga, New Zealand

Be spellbound by a blue light spectacle as you glide down the mystical cave rivers of the Waitomo Caves - created solely by thousands of native glow worms. ♥

MY BUCKETLIST

101 things I want to do with my one wild & precious life

1	24
2	26
3	27
4	28
5	29
6	30
7	31
8	32
9	33
10	34
11	35
12	36
13	37
14	38
15	39
16	40
17	41
18	42
19	43
20	44
21	45
22	46
23	47
24	48

49

50

51

52

53

54

55

56

57

58

59

60

61

62

63

64

65

66

67

68

69

70

71

72

73

74

75

76 ☐

77 ☐

78 ☐

79 ☐

80 ☐

81 ☐

82 ☐

83 ☐

84 ☐

85 ☐

86 ☐

87 ☐

88 ☐

89 ☐

90 ☐

91 ☐

92 ☐

93 ☐

94 ☐

95 ☐

96 ☐

97 ☐

98 ☐

99 ☐

100 ☐

101 ☐

"To live as if we are dying gives us a chance to experience some real presence." - Anne Lammot

Oh *baby*, it's a wild world.

my travels

Asia

Australia

Africa

And in

THE END

it's not the years in your life that count.
It's the life in your years.

- Abraham Lincoln